SMART
PARENTING

SMART PARENTING
A Guide for Parents

Nutan Pandit

Manjul Publishing House

First published in India by

Manjul Publishing House Pvt. Ltd.

Registered Office:
10 Nishat Colony, Bhopal, INDIA-462 003
Corporate Office: 2nd Floor, Usha Preet Complex,
42 Malviya Nagar, Bhopal, INDIA-462 003
E-mail: manjul@manjulindia.com
Website: www.manjulindia.com

Distributed in India by
SV Book Supply Company Pvt. Ltd.
(*a Manjul Company*)
7/32, Ground Floor, Ansari Road, Daryaganj,
New Delhi-110 002 Email: booksupplyco@gmail.com

SMART PARENTING - *A Guide for Parents*
by Nutan Pandit

This edition first published in 2010
Second impression 2012

Copyright © 2010 by Nutan Pandit

ISBN 978-81-8322-182-5

Illustrations by Poonam Sahi

Printed & bound in India by Gopsons Papers Ltd.

This book is for informational purposes only. It is not intended to serve as a substitute for professional advice. The author and publisher specifically disclaim any and all liability arising directly or indirectly from the use of any information contained in this book. Any product mentioned in this book does not imply endorsement of that product by the author or publisher.

All rights reserved. No part of this publication may be reproduced, stored in or introduced into a retrieval system, or transmitted, in any form, or by any means (electronic, mechanical, photocopying, recording or otherwise) without the prior written permission of the publisher. Any person who does any unauthorized act in relation to this publication may be liable to criminal prosecution and civil claims for damages.

This book is dedicated to all those
who are trying to be 'good' parents

CONTENTS

Preface	xi
Becoming a Parent	xv

How Children Behave With Others
Empathy	3
Kindness	7
Fairness and Justice	11
Rights and Responsibilities	15
Sharing and Caring	19
Anger	25
Fear	33

How Parents Influence Children
Think About This	41
Role of the Father in Balancing the New Family Equation	43
Discipline	57
Tackling Indiscipline	65
Spanking	69
Self-Esteem	73
How Do You 'Appear' to Your Child?	79
Love	83
Instant Gratification	89
Your Ambition for Your Child	93
Letting Your Child Be	97
Failure	101
Money Matters	105

Do it Yourself	111
Coping with Tragedy	117
Of Roots and Wings	123
Food Habits	131

Play

Toys	140
Toy Tips	141
Age Zero to One	142
Age One to Three Years	143
Age Three to Six	144
Age Seven to Twelve	146
Teenage	147
Significance of Play	147
Too Much, Too Little and Solitary Play	148

TV, Internet, Gaming

The Internet	158

Video, Computer Games

Digital Demerits	167
Handling Digital Stress	168

Sexuality And Children

Sex as Energy	172
Sex and Adolescents	173
Sex and Society	175
Sexual Changes in Teenagers	175
Sex in the Child	176
Masturbation	177
Preventing Sexual Abuse	179
Signs of Sex Abuse	183
How to Deal with Sex Abuse	184

Talking to Children about Sex 186
Precautions Young Girls and Women Need to
  Take to Keep Stalkers at Bay 188

Environment
Water 195
Litter 196
Shopping 198
Pets 199
Future of Garbage 200

Bibliography 203

References 205

PREFACE

As parents, how you want to bring up your children is entirely your choice. There is no 'right' or 'wrong' way of raising children. However, it is important to decide which way you want to go, and then stick to it. You may find other parents doing things in a way different from yours, and your child may find other children being brought up differently. For instance, some children may have restricted TV hours while others may have free access to the TV. Some children may get a fixed pocket money while others may have unlimited pocket money available to them. Some children may have low-key birthday parties, while others may have lavish ones; some families may travel by train, while others could quite easily afford to travel by air. It is, therefore, important to identify how you are going to do things in your family, and then, explain clearly but firmly to your children how it is going to be for them.

At times, such decisions could be driven by economic considerations, but they could also be conscious, informed and deliberate choices. You can always be open to ideas and suggestions from other people, but it is for you to decide for yourself what suits you and your family the best, and then conform to it with confidence and awareness.

This book will help you make those difficult choices that often confront you. It is written by a parent, for parents, and is largely based on experience, reading, contemplation, as well as common sense. It has been distilled from life, as it has been lived, observed, understood and dealt with in every which way.

This book is also a result of detailed conversations with numerous parents and grandparents on what they thought worked for them, and what they wished they had done differently. There are moments in this book, when the issues it addresses apply more to parents than to children. This is because we, as parents, first need to get our own house in order before we take on the very responsible, pleasurable, and daunting task of being parents!

Most parents strive to do the best for their children, and while, generally, they are usually successful, circumstances often compel them to make compromises. Occasionally, parents may catch themselves—much to their own horror—using the exact words and phrases *their* parents had used with them, even though they may have vowed never to do so!

Many diverse factors eventually go about in shaping a child's personality, which broadly include the home environment, upbringing, siblings, friends, neighbours, teachers, school, the kind of hobbies and non-academic pursuits that the child has, the influence that movies and television have on him and so on and so forth.

Being a parent is a long journey. It is the source of

unadulterated joy, but it will also be fraught with moments of intense anguish. And through it all, you—the parents—will constantly strive to do the right thing for your children.

Here are some beautiful words on what our children will grow up to be:

> *Children are given to us on loan for*
> *A very short period of time.*
> *They come to us like packets of seeds, with no guarantees.*
> *We do not know what they will look like, act like, or have the potential to become.*
> *Our job, like the gardener's, is to meet their needs as best as we can.*
> *To give proper nourishment, love, attention, caring...*
> *and to hope for the best.*

(Source: Kids Publishing World, *Panchkula*.)

BECOMING A PARENT

It is indeed exciting to become a parent. New parents are brimming with ideas on how they plan to bring up their child. Since human infants have a relatively slower rate of physical and mental development, they are dependent on adults for several years after they are born. Every child needs adequate nutrition, protection from environmental hazards along with a positive, stimulating and healthy atmosphere at home and at school, for optimal physical, mental, emotional and spiritual development.

As time goes by, parenting issues are bound to come to the fore. Parents find themselves in a dilemma in trying to get children to behave in a way that is acceptable to them as parents, and to society in general. This can be quite a challenging task, since children are not born socially conditioned. Children are also very spontaneous when it comes to their needs, and will let parents know very clearly when something bothers them; be it hunger, a fight or an argument with a sibling, clothes that they do not like, a lost toy and so on. Parents have to constantly deal with their childrens need's, feelings, frustrations, and yet maintain their equanimity!

Part of the stress when dealing with younger children arises from the fact that adults like a degree of order, routine and manageability in their lives, but children do not understand this and as they grow, their needs and therefore, their routines keep changing. It takes several years of dedicated hard work on the part of the parents to mould their children into adults with well-rounded personalities. This task can be made easier with a little help, some sound advice and proper guidance, which this book hopes to provide.

HOW CHILDREN BEHAVE WITH OTHERS

Bringing up children has gone the whole gamut, from the restrictive disciplining of the 1940s and 1950s, to the permissive and free atmosphere of the 1960s and 1970s, on to the present, more informed, and ostensibly enlightened, method of parenting. The earlier generation was one of disciplinarians, trying to make their children do what was expected of them. The parents in the following generation, having experienced strict discipline in their own growing years, became extra permissive because they were keen not to restrict or thwart their children in any way, so as to let them grow up without complexes of any kind, and hopefully, blossom to their full potential.

It is important for parents to understand that neither the disciplinarian nor the permissive approach to parenting is complete in itself. The former coerces children into doing what is expected of them. Instead of being intimidated, children need to understand why certain things need to be done in a way that ensures a smooth co-existence in society. Say, for instance, we know it is not right to physically assault someone, nor is it right for others to assault us. Or, on a more common level, it is improper to interrupt someone who is speaking, and likewise it is rude of someone to interrupt us when we are talking.

Permissiveness alone, on the other hand, is not good when it comes to raising children. Being left totally directionless and free can actually be very confusing for the child. Children have to be taught and guided to a certain degree, before they are able to make their own choices and take their own decisions. For instance, they have to be taught that it is important to be kind and considerate. While children require some permissiveness for their growth, the amount of guidance they require is much more.

What is required is a happy mix of rules and freedom, and a conscious effort to teach children to be kind, fair and responsible. Each of these traits is concerned with how children treat and behave with others.

EMPATHY

Empathy is an important emotion that should be cultivated in children. It involves sensitising them to other's feelings. Most children are naturally empathetic, and will feel bad over someone else's unhappiness or good about someone's joy. It is rightly said—*Empathy is your pain in my heart.* Children strive to make others feel good, and avoid doing things that may make others feel bad.

Altruism and morality automatically spring from empathy. A recent research by Dr. Felix Warneken of Germany's Max Planck Institute of Evolutionary Anthropology indicates that humans develop the ability for altruism as early as eighteen months of age. His study reported in *Science* (3 March 2006, Volume 311 No. 5765, pp. 1301–3) showed that no other animal is as altruistic as human beings are. Other animals are skilled at co-operating, but do so to achieve a goal, for example, banding together to chase down food or for protection against predators and so on. Warneken performed a series of ordinary tasks in front of a group of toddlers, such as hanging towels with clothespins or stacking books. He pretended to sometimes 'struggle' with the tasks by deliberately messing up—either by dropping clothespins or knocking over a pile of books. Over and over, each of twenty-four toddlers offered help within seconds—but only if he appeared to need it. Videos show how one over-all clad baby glanced from Warneken's face to the dropped clothespins, before quickly crawling over and grabbing the object, then pushing up to his feet and eagerly handing back the pin.

Warneken never asked for help and nor did he say 'thank you', so as not to taint the research by training youngsters to expect praise if they helped. After all, altruism means helping without expecting anything in return. The toddlers, interestingly, didn't bother to offer help when Warneken deliberately pulled a book off the stack or threw a clothespin to the floor. To be altruistic, babies must have the cognitive ability to understand other people's goals, plus possess what Warneken calls 'pro-social motivation'.

A toddler's endearing desire to help out actually implies fairly sophisticated brain development. This is a trait that is of interest to anthropologists trying to get to the root of altruism and co-operation in the evolutionary process.

We can teach our children altruistic behaviour by teaching them to respect people older than them, especially the elderly and to be sensitive to their needs. Likewise, they can be taught to be kind to animals, and taught not to make fun of others if they are somewhat differently abled.

In turn, parents should also treat children with empathy. Even if a child has a shortcoming, the parents should show unconditional love to the child. The child should be taught to be as normal as possible. The problem should not be suppressed, but discussed in an open and normal way. Domestic help should be told not to take jibes at the child. Teachers should be informed to give extra attention to the child, and protect the child from being picked on by other children.

KINDNESS

The renowned psychoanalyst Sigmund Freud saw man as totally selfish, self-centred and uncaring. He felt that the kindly traits a person displayed were a result of civilised training provided by parents and society. However, in 1979 a team of psychologists observed twenty-six preschoolers aged between three and five years. The children were observed during thirty hours of free play-time. The results showed that the children engaged in approximately 1,200 kind actions like comforting, helping, co-operating, sharing, and so on. It was the so called 'civilising forces'—parents and society—that often made them develop prejudices. Thus, caring seems to be a natural trait of human character, just like aggression.

We need our children to be kind to others. It is a fact that by reducing another person's pain or giving someone else pleasure, we receive great joy. According to psychologist Robert Weiss easing someone's pain is in itself an effective positive reinforcer. He found that people work harder and faster at a job when their only pay-off is reducing the discomfort of someone they've never even met before.

A study conducted at the University of Iowa, USA, showed that the most effective way of dealing with anger is to help someone else. It was proved to be more effective than giving vent to one's anger by boxing a punching bag, which still leaves the person angry. In contrast, helping someone can leave you feeling calm.

Therefore, developing a kind nature in a child will immensely benefit him in the long run, contributing greatly to his general well-being. It is also more in harmony with the more positive innate human tendencies.

In the words of the American author Mark Twain: 'The best way to cheer yourself up is to cheer somebody else up.'

FAIRNESS AND JUSTICE

Children should be taught to treat others without prejudice or favouritism. They should be made to learn that the same rules apply to everyone. That everyone, for instance, shares the burden and responsibility for the welfare of the smooth running of society, of one's home and the school.

The reason for this is clearly elucidated in the following quote by a German clergyman of the Nazi era:

'In Germany they first came to get the communists, and I didn't speak up because I wasn't a communist. Then they came for the Jews, and I didn't speak up because I wasn't a Jew. Then they came for the trade unionists, and I didn't speak up because I wasn't a trade unionist. Then they came for the Catholics, and I didn't speak up because I was a Protestant. Then they came for me. And by that time no one was left to speak up for me.' (Writings by Daisaku Ikeda, President, Soka Gakkai International).

An important part of justice and fairness is clarity. This was discussed by the yogi and founder of the Isha Foundation, Sadhguru Jaggi Vasudev in January 2007 at the first World Convention on Science and Spirituality in New Delhi. He said that clarity is more important than confidence. If you imagine you can see God, it can give you confidence, but it cannot give you clarity. Confidence without clarity is disastrous. For instance, if you are driving a car with a lot of confidence, but no clarity, it could be disastrous.

He further said that if you do something foolish and wrong, your intelligence will bother you. However, if you do something foolish and wrong and have the confidence that God wants you to do it, your intelligence will not bother you. You will have the confidence that it is heaven endorsed! Clarity is, therefore, of utmost importance. This could equally apply to terrorists who might kill freely believing it is what God wants them to do.

RIGHTS AND RESPONSIBILITIES

If a bird has to lay eggs, she will first build a nest. In cold countries, squirrels work harder in the summer months to store nuts and seeds so that they have food in the winter. A child should be made to realise that with rights, come responsibilities. Those who are responsible work harder and realise that they need to fulfil certain duties. For instance, if you want to get married and have a family you need to be consistent in your work. In fact, you need to work to sustain yourself even if you do not want to start a family. It is only irresponsible people who expect to be taken care of by parents or others in their adulthood. People who shirk responsibility mostly blame others for their failure to take responsibility, and are also very critical of those who do. It is, therefore, very important to inculcate responsibility in children, at the individual, family and social level. At the individual level, the child can be taught to keep his possessions neatly. For example, you may say, 'Put your crayons back in the box after you finish using them.' Or, on a personal level, it can be 'Keep yourself neat and clean,' 'Bathe regularly and comb your hair,' or 'Wash your hands before eating.' At the family level, the child can help in laying the table or clearing it. At the community level, the child can be taught to obey traffic rules so that there is safety on the roads. The child can be taught that if people want good governance, they need to actively vote for and support the right person, which will be an example of teaching responsibility at the political level.

On a more mundane level, involving the child in tidying the room or study table, and appreciating his effort with an 'Oh! That looks nice!' will teach him that this behaviour is desirable and results in a neat and pleasant environment. A child could be made to learn a few rules repeatedly towards achievement of this goal, for instance, 'Put your shoes on the shoe rack after you've taken them off,' 'Put your dirty socks in the laundry basket when you return from school,' and so on.

Also, a child should learn to finish his homework on a regular basis. If he is careless, it could set him back in school work, resulting in catching up to do during holidays or at play time. It could also create a tense atmosphere at home. Finishing his homework or otherwise acting responsibly should never be linked to the child getting a gift or any other incentive in return. It is a good idea to instruct children to finish their homework all by themselves as soon as they get home, so that they can relax for the rest of the day, doing whatever they feel like.

If you insist that your child does his homework in your presence, you are making the child dependent on you. You are also inadvertently discouraging him from taking up a responsibility. In as many matters as you can, be it homework, brushing teeth at night, setting the school bag according to the next day's timetable, etc., encourage the child to do things by himself. This will set a general trend towards responsible habits.

Gradually inculcate responsibility for every possible routine in the house. For instance, say things like, 'It is very important to eat a good breakfast because it has been quite some time since we ate dinner last night', or, 'Our system needs to kick-start in the morning with a good, healthy breakfast'.

When a child understands why we do certain things, he will be more co-operative. He should not be made to feel that things need to be done because there are rewards or brownie points to be gained. On the other hand, do not threaten him with punishment either. As far as possible, try and explain to children why we need to do things the way we do them, be it cleaning, bathing, sleeping, or a more complicated chore. You could explain, for example, that we need sleep, because our body works better when rested. Or that we need to keep ourselves clean by bathing, otherwise one can get skin irritations and bad body odour.

Also, it is a good idea to teach children that they have a responsibility to take action in any area of their life with which they feel dissatisfied. If they feel they need more pocket money, they should think of ways to earn it. If they want to have different kinds of food once in a while, they can either help in setting the menu or experiment with cooking it themselves. Children should be discouraged from complaining. If they do complain, you could say to them, 'What do you think can be done about it?' This will set them thinking in the right direction.

SHARING AND CARING

There is an Irish proverb that states: 'It is in the shelter of each other that people live.'

Sharing within the family is very important—and for sharing to happen, lines of communication should always be open. Family members should make it a point to always speak to each other about how their day was and how they feel about it. It is extremely important that you know your child's friends, and also acquaint your child with your friends. You should spend a considerable amount of time in each other's company, without the presence of outsiders. This should preferably be a leisurely, relaxed time without too many rules, constraints or a very strict timetable. It should be time spent to bond with each other. When children know that someone cares about them, they acquire a sense of security, which eventually helps them in the long run. As they say, the stronger and steadier the bow, the further will the arrow reach.

Unfortunately, modern lifestyles are leading to a decline in the concept of sharing and caring. As the demands on children increase, it leaves them with lesser and lesser time for fun activities and trivial pursuits or maybe just spending time with a family member who is wise or simply fun to be with! Birthday parties these days are more stress than pleasure, what with event managers organising them for you, if you so wish. Parents and children both vie to have a better party than their friends, and all this hoopla takes away the spontaneity of this very special occasion! What is more important is that children have fun at a party. The messier they get, the more fun they have! Children can have as much fun in a garden or a park as in an air conditioned hall. They can enjoy a home-made cake just as much as a fancy made-to-order cake, and they can look good in fairly regular clothes. All they need is good cheer to carry it off!

In order that children inculcate the right values, they should be taught to appreciate and value others, irrespective of their stature. They should learn to genuinely accept others as fellow individuals; everyone craves acceptance, attention and affection, and these are received as much as they are given back.

Another important trait that children must develop is the habit of extending a helping hand to someone in need. There are times in the lives of each one of us when a personal or professional crisis overwhelms us. During such times a hand of support always helps tide over the crisis in a quicker and better manner. Also, this trait will help your children generate a lot of goodwill, and they will in turn get help and support easily in their times of need. Helping others feels good, and, as the American poet and philosopher Ralph Waldo Emerson put it, 'Happiness is a perfume you cannot pour on others without getting a few drops on yourself.'

Children should be taught to show that they care by being in constant touch with those who are dear to them. Sending out cards or wishing people over the phone or via email on their special days is a great way to do this, as is meeting up with them and their families whenever possible. We all share a special bond with people we are connected with or grew up with. Such bonds must be nurtured and strengthened. Your children should be made to realise that life is not an inanimate, passive journey, with money-making as its only aim. It is about how one lives it, the warmth that one spreads around, and about how one makes others feel acknowledged, appreciated, and respected.

When something unpleasant happens to someone we know, we should not cut ourselves off from them. Instead, we should make an effort to stay in touch and, although some of us may find it difficult to express ourselves, we can surely enquire how they are feeling and coping with their loss or unhappy situation. We should not act as though nothing has happened. When someone is grieving, we should reach out and ask them if we can do anything to help. You can offer to help them with paper work, legal hurdles, or anything else that may seem burdensome to them at that point of time. You could call or email them without asking for a health update if they are ill, or groping for some gossip if, say, their family is breaking up. You should just call to ask how they are doing, and tell them that you are with them in this moment of stress. You should concentrate on their feelings rather than yours. Care should be taken not to lecture or to pass judgment in such situations. The person in question should be encouraged to talk so that he can work through his grief. The fact that everyone reacts differently when under stress should be respected. For instance, some people may want to talk about it, while others may simply clamp up. Others may go off food completely, while still others may start overeating. We must, therefore, be senitive enough to handle any given situation.

In case of bereavement, everyone needs personal grieving time. This could at times extend up to a year, or even several years in some cases. This should be respected, and pressure should not be mounted to rush the person grieving to come out of it. However, it is unnatural and unhealthy when someone grieves beyond a reasonable period. If they do, they may need counselling, and perhaps even psychiatric help. Homoeopathic medicines or complementary systems of healing can also help.

ANGER

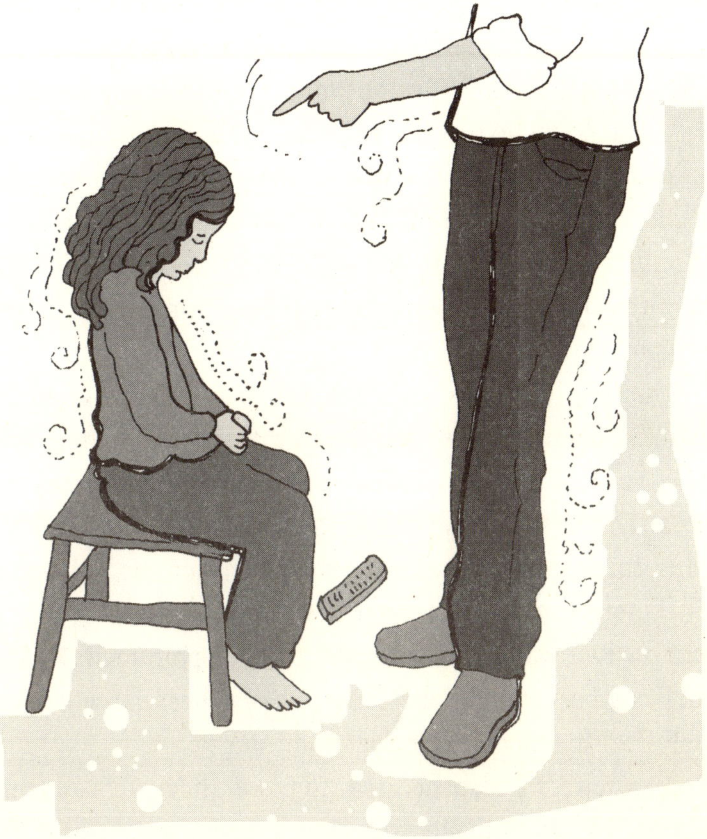

Sometimes anger may be experienced out of fear. For example, if your child suddenly darts across a busy street, or plays a prank by hiding from you, the fear you experience for the child's safety can make you very anxious, and therefore, angry. This fear will stem from your concern that your child may be hurt by a speeding vehicle, or that he may be kidnapped. If this happens, you should explain clearly and firmly to your child the reasons for your anger. Explain that carefully looking towards the right and left to check for oncoming traffic before crossing the road is an extremely important habit. Or, that it is mandatory for you to know that the child is safe because if something were the matter, you would need to mobilise help, and maybe call up the police. Telling your child that fear often makes people angry will be an important lesson for your child.

There will be times when the child may experience anger. Learning about fairness has the power to reduce anger in a child. For instance, if a child learns that at school everyone has a right to the swing or see-saw, he may be disappointed if his turn does not come at break-time or the bell rings just before his turn. In such a situation, the child might react in two ways—either anger or disappointment. If the child has been taught the concept of fairness he will most likely feel disappointed rather than angry.

Children can also become angry if they are suddenly deprived of something long cherished, due to an unavoidable reason. For instance, it could be a family holiday getting cancelled at the last minute due to a serious illness of a grandparent. Such a situation can frustrate and upset children, especially if they have already shared their plans with their friends. You shouldn't react with anger to your child's negative reaction but allow him to have his initial outburst. There is a lot for your child to learn here. Make sure to tell your child exactly what you are feeling... sad at your child's disappointment, but also angry at his insensitivity and self-centerdness.

Saying something to the effect, 'Do you realise what grandma/pa is going through? Have you thought of the fear and helplessness s/he must have felt when she had that heart attack?' or, 'Remember, grandma/pa is my mother/father. S/he was there for me through all my growing years and I am responsible for her/him, as I am for you!' will help him see things in the right perspective. You should ask the child to go and think about it all by himself. It is very likely that he will come to you after sometime and say how sorry he is, and that he wants grandma/pa to know that he is there for her/him! Children willingly offer help and support, once they are made to understand the situation.

Children should be made to understand that the world does not exist to fulfil all their needs alone. Sometimes they may not get what they want because others may have an equal claim to it, or because it will infringe on other people's rights or well-being. This is an important lesson by which we can raise children with well-rounded and balanced personalities. This will help keep children out of trouble as they grow into adulthood. We know from newspapers that many crimes are committed by individuals frustrated at not getting their own way, be it instances of road rage, or sometimes even murder!

Some men may be aggressive because they feel that it is macho to be aggressive while putting their point across. Others may feel that aggression with family members establishes authority. However, it is important to realise that aggression in the family cannot solve problems. It only complicates matters further by creating a tense atmosphere of fear and destructiveness, and destroys relationships. Children must be told to work at handling a problem, not manhandling someone to solve it.

However, at times anger can be well justified and legitimate. Children should not be made to feel guilty about getting angry. Anger is a legitimate response to injustice, and should be used when required to assert oneself. Children should not get bullied into submission because they cannot stand up for themselves.

Always discourage your child from hitting others when feeling angry. Although the child's anger may be legitimate, his aggression will only result in a vicious cycle of hate and revenge, without solving anything. It could sometimes also result in an act of extreme aggression arising out of a moment of madness, the aftermath of which could ruin the child's future.

Telling the child that you would be disappointed at an aggressive reaction from him should drive home the point.

On a humanitarian level, ask your child to try and think what she would feel on being hit. When you give such a firm message to your child, you will nurture a person who will not hurt others.

This certainly does not mean that others can freely bully your child, and that your child should meekly accept irrational behaviour from others. Your child must be told to always remember his strength. If being hit unfairly, children must know how to assertively protect themselves from injury or injustice. They need to be made to understand that if they do not stand up for themselves and object to unfair treatment, others will see no reason to change their behaviour. Children need to be assertive and tactfully draw a line so people can understand that though they are not needlessly aggressive, they cannot be taken undue advantage of.

Anger normally begets anger. For instance, if you happen to scold your child in the morning, he would most likely let loose his temper at a friend in school. His friend in turn, might kick a dog in frustration. It becomes a vicious cycle. Most of the time, anger is misplaced.

If you have had a rough day at work, and your family members remark that you are looking upset, you can simply state the facts in a calm and rational way. You could say, 'Sorry, I am thinking about the golden handshake (voluntary retirement) offer that was made to me at work today.' Or, 'I don't think I imagined it, but each time I called for the peon today, he was busy doing something else.' Then work out your anger by either taking a long walk, listening to music, or doing small chores around the house. If, instead, you have an outburst on the family members, say nasty things you do not actually mean, bang doors, sulk etc. no one will take you seriously. When you don't communicate clearly, no one will know what is bugging you. Not even yourself!

A very good way to handle a problem is to remain calm and not get angry. You should instead focus on the problem and how to best solve it. Concentrating on the problem at hand can help you to avoid getting into arguments, or hitting out at people in a fit of rage, which only clouds your ability to think rationally. It can also lead to passionate outbursts or actions like physical assault, which could cause injury to someone. It could also lead you to say things you might later regret.

There are a few simple steps to anger management. First, you must identify and define the problem, staying calm as you do so. For example, if your child is not completing his homework on a regular basis and this makes you angry, you'd first have to recognise the fact that you are angry, and pinpoint the reason for this anger. It is important that you also show some understanding, saying, 'I can understand that playing or talking on the phone is more fun than doing homework,' and then talking of how you feel, in a practical, no-nonsense manner. The plainspeak will convey the message clearly.

It is not advisable that you comment on the child's character, or be excessively negative. Children whose feelings are respected are likely to respect the feelings of others. It would be better to say something like, 'I feel you require constant policing to make sure you don't make this a habit, and also so that it does not lead you steadily downhill' would be a much better than saying, for example, 'I have had it with you ... take it from me—your future is doomed!' You can further state the action you plan to take. For example, 'Henceforth, you will first complete your homework after returning from school, before you do anything else.'

Angry grudges held within the heart fester like wounds, and corrode from inside. They are not worth nursing. Forgiving and carrying on with life is always the best option. The greatest gift one can give oneself is that of forgiveness. When you are hurt, you often say that you cannot forgive and forget. It's okay to forgive and not forget. When you hold back forgiveness you are often very judgemental and strict with yourself too. You may carry a heavy burden of guilt for a perceived wrong committed by you. When you forgive others, you also find it easier to forgive yourself either now or in the future. To start with, it is enough to say to someone that you forgive them, whether you mean it or not, and then divert your mind to something else. Over a period of time the hurt will lessen, or at least not cripple you into depression since you will be distracting yourself from the pain by concentrating on another activity.

FEAR

Fear experienced by children should never be dismissed with, 'Oh, don't be silly!' It should always be acknowledged, addressed and dealt with. For a child, fears can be very real. Anything new or strange can scare a little child, for instance, a dog, darkness, etc. In older children, it could have a larger manifestation, say for example, the fear of losing a parent, or joining a new school, etc.

If your child is afraid of the dark, you may either leave a night light on in his room, and also tell him that he can come to you, if he's still afraid. An interesting incident illustrating how fears can be addressed comes to mind. Once a toddler visiting my home got terribly scared when he came face to face with my pet dog, Sheru (a Dobermann). The tall black dog was almost the same height as the little boy.

In order that the little boy should not develop a life-long fear of dogs, I baked him a cake and sent it to him with a little note from the dog!

The note said:

Dear Gautam,

I hope you enjoy this cake. My mom made it for you. I am sorry I frightened you the other day when you came to my house. I don't know why God has given me such a scary face. Sometimes, even people as old as your mom and dad get scared when they see me!

I enjoyed meeting you, so do come over again. I promise I will not bite.

Love,
Sheru.

This worked wonderfully, and little Gautam readily visited us from then on!

Sometimes, a child may be scared of an imaginary monster under her bed. To counter this, you can take a room freshner and spray it under the bed pretending it to be monster repellant. You could then flash a light under the bed to confirm to the child that the monster is gone.

A child's fears should never be mocked or belittled. If a child is afraid and unsure, it is a very real fear. Or, if a child is leaving for boarding school and says that he does not want to go 'because I will miss you,' it is not something that should be taken lightly.

In situations where the parents are going through a divorce, the children are bound to be afraid. In such a situation, a joint family could be an oasis of security for these children as they will feel less insecure because there will always be someone older to provide love and security, and also someone of about the same age, like cousins, who they can probably speak with about their fears.

Fear could sometimes be instigated or magnified by television. For example, if there is news that a killer is at large in the city, the child will fear that the killer may come to the house and get him. If the TV announces natural disasters like tornadoes, floods etc, the child may fear being struck by them. Studies confirm that children who watch a lot of television tend to be exposed to more violence and thus feel more insecure than those who don't.

According to psychologist Yamamoto, 'All too often, we don't see or hear what is really troubling our children.' A survey done by him shows that children are afraid of losing face; and being thought of as unattractive, stupid or dishonest. For them, it is more troubling to wet their pants in class, get a bad report card or repeat a year, for example, than it is to undergo surgery or be confronted by a rival brother or sister—situations a parent might expect to be more disconcerting. For a child, a blow to his self-esteem is a terrible thing to endure.

Yamamoto's studies make it clear that children need to be accepted by their friends. A parent should take a child's complaint about being teased, left out of games or not being invited to a party very seriously. The sense that you are there, 'providing an anchor' as Yamamoto puts it, will give your child the much needed confidence and help the child to adjust to living in society.

No fear should be allowed to take on a huge dimension. If that happens, it will stunt the child's growth, limit his achievements and make the child lead life to a minimum, rather than to a fearless maximum.

'Learn from the past.
Do not come to the end of life
Only to find you have not lived.
For many may come to the point of leaving the
Space of the earth
And when they gaze back,
They see the joys and the beauty
That could not be theirs because
Of the fears they lived.'

—CLEARWATER

HOW PARENTS INFLUENCE CHILDREN

THINK ABOUT THIS

If a child
Lives with criticism
He learns to condemn.
If a child lives with hostility
He learns to fight.
If a child lives with ridicule
He learns to be shy.
If a child lives with shame
He learns to feel guilty.

If a child lives with tolerance
He learns to be patient.
If a child lives with encouragement
He learns to appreciate.
If a child lives with fairness
He learns justice.

If a child lives with security
He learns to have faith.
If a child lives with approval
He learns to like himself.
If a child lives with acceptance and friendship
He learns to give love in the world.

(Source: Text attributed to The English Nursery School at The Hague, Netherlands)

ROLE OF THE FATHER IN BALANCING THE NEW FAMILY EQUATION

It is said that the only thing permanent in life is change! Undoubtedly, it is amazing how life takes a little boy through the journey of adulthood, marriage and then to fatherhood. Although being parents makes a couple feel an all consuming responsibility, it is important that they do not become too child centric. They also need to cater to their personal needs. They should continue to take time out for themselves and for each other. Children should be taught not to interrupt when parents are talking. Just a brief, 'Please do not interrupt when I am talking to mummy' in a soft voice should suffice. It is important to let your children know that you are special to each other and need a zone of privacy.

There is a possibility that if everything revolves around the child, one or the other parent may start to feel that their relationship as a couple has become secondary. Besides, the child will develop a bloated sense of self-importance. As a result, when that importance is not there for him when he ventures out into the real, adult world, he will find it difficult to cope. Unnecessarily, the 'child' in him may feel ignored by colleagues, bosses, or peers, when actually, the behaviour of others may be entirely normal.

At the other extreme, if a child is ignored at home and not given the attention that he requires, it could mar the child's personality. Such a child may either resort to exaggerated attention-seeking behaviour, or may become withdrawn. A child who withdraws can become very uncomfortable when he receives normal attention, and will shy away. Such a child can miss many opportunities for developing a healthy and positive personality. Children, therefore, require the correct balance of attention and being left to themselves.

As parents, we also need to teach by example. For instance, if we do not want our children to interrupt us when we speak we shouldn't be interrupting them when they speak either. Besides, when we want our children to learn to take responsibility for what they say and do, we should strive to do the same ourselves.

Relationships need to be well-balanced to be healthy. Imbalances like over-gratefulness to your parents, over-involvement with your child or your wife; or totally ignoring your parents can result in stressed relationships, which will definitely affect the child adversly. Communication and dialogue is the key to maintaining this balance.

Fathers should remember to keep a balance and not focus their attention only on the baby or on work. Apart from this, they must also nurture their relationship with their spouse. According to a study published in *The Journal of Personality and Social Psychology* (December 2006): 'The way a person responds to a partner's good fortune—with excitement or passive approval, shared pride or indifference is the most crucial factor in tightening the bond between a couple or undermining it.'

A couple should never give up communicating with each other. When either of the partners do that and goes into a sulk, a cold, lasting chill can slowly creep into the relationship. All relationships have to be worked upon.

For some people it is very important to withdraw and be in their own space for a while after an argument. The other spouse should respect that, but couples should, as a rule, make up before going to bed at night. Never sleep over a fight; even if you just hold your partner's hand.

When you talk, try and establish ground rules like, the first part is simply letting off steam. For instance, 'You made lousy dinner/you forgot my mom's birthday!!/your mom must always have her room cleaned first, and that bothers me/you came home so late again!' Talk without apportioning blame. 'I feel awful when you get home so late. If you call or message I'll feel better. Sorry to miss your mom's birthday. Next time it will help if you remind me. I have so much on my mind that I tend to forget.'

Or talk about your feelings. 'I don't like it when your mom insists that the cleaning lady cleans her room first. Since I have to lock my cleaned room before I leave, I get late for my appointments.'

Remember you don't need to give solutions. When someone talks of what bothers them, they do not expect an on-the-spot solution. So, you don't need to fire the chauffeur if your wife is complaining about him!

However, knowing each other's mind will help. It will help to establish harmony eventually, because you will be able to make wise decisions. For instance, if you both like to eat good food at home, you can decide to make your lives simpler by getting a good cook, or trying out recipes together. Since remembering birthdays is such an issue, you can tie up with the local florist. Give him annual orders, so that throughout the year, on the relevant dates, he sends flowers to the relevant people with your card attached to the bouquet.

Culture practices and advertisements always reflect the values of that society.

I remember an advertisement from when I was young. It showed a father reading the newspaper, and a mother chasing a little child running all over the place with a spoonful of food in her hand. The father, on hearing the noise lowers his newspaper, glances at this scene before him, smiles and returns to his newspaper! The advertisements of today have undergone a sea-change. We have 'Raymond, the Complete Man', which shows a man who is not shy to show he cares, and is sensitive to the emotions of his little daughter who is waiting for him to return home from work. He is shown to be playful and caring towards a little puppy. No longer is a man considered a sissy or henpecked if he openly displays his emotions.

In fact, the totally aggressive man is passé. Today, we are living in a civilised society in which every human being is respected, where we are learning that we also need to respect the earth, nature, wildlife and the environment, etc. This is a new age of humanism, compassion, love, justice and equality.

The old school of thought prescribed certain traits and abilities to be either male or masculine, and others to be female or feminine. Female abilities were principally considered to be cooking, parenting, being intuitive, being sensitive and generally nurturing. Masculine abilities were to be assertive, having a better mathematical, logical and navigational perception, and having the ability for critical thinking, and so on.

The new thinking is that traits are neither male nor female. Traits do not have genders, people do. So it is quite okay if, for example, you wake your wife up with a cup of tea in bed, and then make the bed as she prepares breakfast. Such gestures will make for a loving home environment.

Children learn faster by example. When they observe both parents diligently doing their part in the house, they will also want to do the same. You should encourage your children to chip in by helping out around the house in whatever way they can—to lay the dinner table or clear it; fold or iron the laundry, etc. When everyone chips in, household chores do not become insurmountable mountains that sap you of time and energy. They become divided into do-able tasks that are shared by all; the house gets managed more easily and is a more comfortable home.

A woman, who is primarily a homemaker, needs greater assurance that her opinion matters and her decisions are taken seriously. Extra attention should be put in by the spouse to bolster her self-esteem. The mother's image in the house should never be that of a suffering household help.

Some mothers who are constantly criticised as being inefficient mothers or bad housekeepers, or otherwise made to feel unloved, could well slip into depression. If the woman is expected to do all the work alone, she will gradually lose her energy and enthusiasm, and will be left exhausted and deflated. She needs to be praised, appreciated, and thanked, and the family needs to be of help to her instead of making unreasonable demands on her. Just as she always provides love and nurturing to the family she also requires caring from the family in return. It is rightly said, 'You can give only what you have.' A happy person will unwittingly spread happiness and a sad person will likewise spread sadness.

This particularly holds true when a woman is a new mother, having only just delivered a baby. There is a condition called postpartum depression which means depression that affects a woman after the birth of a baby. In order for a new mother not to suffer from it, she needs lots of love, care and support. In the joint family setup, there used to be abundant support for the mother. Today, couples often move away from home to work, to make a statement of their independence, or for other reasons, and consequently miss out on the many advantages of a joint family set-up when children are being raised.

For instance, it is always possible to have the supervision of a family member over the children apart from maids, so that the upbringing of children is not entirely influenced by the maids or other care givers. Grandparents can instil values in children, apart from supervising on other small but important things like making sure they wash their hands before they eat, helping them with homework, supervising them as they play or study, and provide a sense of security if the parents are at work, and so on.

However, today, in spite of joint families, couples may still feel the load, since the grandparents may have a busy social and work life themselves. Further, there are no more aunts, uncles or other elders living with the families, who could actively participate in child rearing.

In such a scenario, the mother needs the support of her spouse. A new mother is generally sleep-deprived as she breastfeeds round the clock at approximately two to three hour intervals. Over a period of days, this can be very taxing. She may start to feel irritable due to sleep deprivation.

So, how can Dad help?

(1) Dad can help with household chores, especially when the household help is absent or on leave.

(2) It is important to appreciate the efforts that the mother puts into the care of the baby. Do not let it bother you if on some days some household chores like dusting or cooking do not get done. If that is so, Dad can help with the laundry or the dusting, cook, or make a sandwich or order food from a take-away.

(3) Whenever Dad gets home, he could take over babysitting for one or two hours, so that the mother can get time for herself. She could relax by doing whatever she wishes—sleeping, visiting a neighbour, going to the market, anything. It would give her time to recharge her batteries. The father could also be tired from a full day at work. So, he could simply

lie down and place the baby on his chest or next to him and play with the baby.

(4) When problems crop up, say, if the baby is unwell or hurt, or if the staff has suddenly left, neither parent should blame the other or anybody else. These are common irritants that are basically non-issues which need special attention to be diffused so as to prevent them from escalating into major issues. One has to address and resolve such matters without either side losing face, taking care not to make it a prestige issue. So, when such a crisis presents itself, do what needs to be done in a detached sort of way and get on with your life.

(5) To help the mother get enough sleep, the father can feed the baby with expressed breast milk at night so that the mother can sleep through one feed and get at least about four hours of undisturbed sleep.

A mother may ask 'How does one express breast milk?' One can express breast milk manually that is, with one's hands. It's best to express when breastfeeding, since the flow of milk is already established. One can express the milk remaining in the breast the baby was feeding from, and did not empty completely. Or, one can express from the side the baby did not feed from. In order to express milk the mother should place four fingers under the breast, with the little finger touching the chest wall. The thumb is to be placed on the top portion of the breast where the normal colour of skin and the dark colour of skin meet. The breast should then be pressed and the milk that is thus released should be collected in a stainless steel bowl that has a smooth rounded edge. It should have a capacity of 250 ml. or more. Never press the nipple, it could hurt. If the breasts are leaking milk that is another good time to express milk. The milk will stay un-spoilt at room temperature for six to eight hours, even in hot summer months.

One can also use a battery-operated or a manual breast pump, in which case all parts used will have to be properly sterilised by boiling, since one cannot scrub clean the sticky film of milk that settles on the base of such equipment, forming a breeding ground for germs. Do not use sterilising solutions; babies get used to their smell and will not have milk if the smell is absent. Besides, we must not have the baby ingest a daily dose of sterilising solution. Another disadvantage of such equipment is that it is made of plastic, which is known to leak a chemical and estrogen hormone into any liquid present in it.

The father may wonder how to feed expressed breast milk to the baby. In order to feed the baby, the baby needs to be placed with the head slightly raised on the father's lap. Then the father needs to take the bowl of milk and place its edge at the baby's lower lip and tilt till the level of milk reaches the lips of the baby. The baby will sense its presence and lap it up by sticking its tongue out, just like a puppy or a dog slurps up milk or water by sticking its tongue out. When the level of the milk goes down, tilt some more. Initially, if given to a baby who has already had a bottle, the baby is likely to protest by flailing its arms. Some milk might spill, so make the baby wear a bib before trying it for the first time, or ask someone to hold the baby's arms. The alternative would be to swaddle the baby or wrap it in a sheet so that it does not flail its arms. Gradually, the baby will become adept at it.

Feeding from a bowl is best because the baby's tongue moves exactly as when breastfeeding. Besides, the baby needs to make an effort for every sip it takes, so it does not get used to over-feeding.

When given the bottle, the baby may suffer from nipple confusion and start rejecting the breast. If feeding from the bowl is difficult, the father can feed with a spoon.

THE "PRESENT" FATHER

Child psychologist Lee Salk says: 'The material success of parents can become a detriment to child-raising if it comes at the expense of time that could be spent with their children. Children can tell fairly young what their parents consider important. If they see everything comes ahead of them, there is likely to be trouble ahead.' Wise fathers know that relationships, not material things, bring satisfaction in life. Men striving to do the best for their children are open to learning. They are always on the lookout for healthy role models. 'Effective fathers know they need support and aren't afraid to ask for it,' says Paul Lewis, author of *The Five Key Habits of Smart Dads: A Powerful Strategy for Successful Fathering.* 'They talk to other fathers and perhaps choose one as a role model or mentor.'

One of the ways in which fathers can be involved with their children is by helping with homework, attending parent-teacher meetings, playing games, spending time with each child and generally spending more time at home.

Pediatrician T. Berry Brazelton says, 'Everything we know shows that when men are involved with their children, the children's I.Q. increases by the time they are six or seven.' He further says that when a father is involved 'the child is likely to have a sense of humor, to develop a sort of inner excitement, to believe in himself or herself, to be more motivated to learn.'

A father keeping an emotional distance can have a negative effect. According to Dr L.B. Silverstein of New York University: 'Research clearly documents the direct correlation between a father's absence and higher rates of aggressive behavior in sons, sexually precocious behavior in daughters, and more rigid sex stereotypes in children of both sexes.'

Ken R. Canfield, author of *The 7 Secrets of Effective Fathers: Becoming the Father Your Children Need*, surveyed 4,000 men to determine what contributes to effective fathering. As a result of his studies, he discovered that a good father knew the following specifics about his child.

- When his child had a difficult day
- When his child was upset about something
- The names of his child's best friends
- What encouraged his child the most
- When he had hurt the child's feelings
- His child's strength and weaknesses

- What motivated his child
- When his child was embarrassed
- Most of his child's recent disappointing experiences

DISCIPLINE

It is important to discipline children with fixed boundaries and routines set for them. Children who live with rules, boundaries or structures may not like them and may complain about them, but the fact is that they feel very secure as a result of them. They remember them with a lot of fondness when they are grown up. So, do not feel that you are being a tyrant by disciplining your child. In an effort to be a good friend to your child, do not ignore discipline. They need parents who they can look up to for direction.

Children lack judgement and experience. Dr. Barton Schmitt, a professor of paediatrics warns, 'The more democratic you are in the early years, the more demanding and spoiled kids become.' It should be clear to children that yours is the final word. Older children can discuss rules and the reasoning behind them, or express their opinions about certain rules, but they have to eventually respect the rules laid down by the parents. Of course, very small children, toddlers for instance, may simply be told, 'because I say so.'

Slightly older children may want to see violent movies or buy expensive designer clothes, because, 'All the other kids have watched it (or have them).' Your response to this should be, 'Sorry, not in this house.' You and your spouse need to be firm on this together. Your child will learn the important lesson that sometimes you have to do without some things, and it's best for them to take this in their stride.

When you draw the line on your child's demands, you must have the confidence and conviction to convey your refusal in a manner that is effective. You as the parent have the right to say a firm 'no'. If some of your child's friends have expensive clothes, shoes and toys, the latest in mobile phones, expensive cars, and so on, and your child too hankers after those things, you do not become a bad parent if you refuse your child's demands.

Be confident of your decision, not apologetic about it. Refuse firmly without raising your voice. Do not give in because you feel guilty of not spending enough time or doing enough for your child. Explain to your child why you are refusing (for example, it would be a waste of money, or, wearing a designer label is not going to make a difference to the child's personality or future prospects etc. You can get regular clothes that resemble designer clothes and come at a fraction of the cost. With a little imagination/trial and error, you can turn out an outfit as stunning as designer clothes). This will make your child really value good things when she gets them. Remember, you are not being a tyrant here. Getting everything too early in life would leave nothing for the child to look forward to. As a result, there will be no joy left in life.

After the ground rules have been set, allow and encourage children to take decisions within those ground rules. For instance, the good habit of bathing daily must be enforced by you, but whether the child wants to bathe in the morning or in the evening can be left to him to decide. There is, thus, a choice on when to bathe, but there is no choice on whether to bathe or not. You say to the child, 'When will you have a bath?' and not, 'Would you like to have a bath?'

There will be times when the child will not want to follow the rules. For instance, it is important for the child to follow a fixed bedtime because it gets the child used to a regular routine, which is always good. It also gives parents private time for themselves. But sometimes when having a great time, the child may want to ignore her bedtime. At such times you can use a very stern voice that makes the child realise that you mean business. It should be a low, stern tone saved only for such times. You can also use the stern tone when the child is throwing a tantrum, screaming and shouting at a party or in a shop. It could be further used when setting limits in unfamiliar surroundings, like airports or other public places where you need to give important instructions like, 'Hold my hand' or, 'Stay close to me.'

When disciplining the child, it is important to explain why a certain kind of behaviour is expected of him. For instance, when the father comes home, he should be asked if he wants to catch up with the news before the child switches on the programme of his choice. Or, if there are four children and one tricycle for everyone to get a ride, you should allow each child to ride it for five to ten minutes. When the child follows these instructions, you should reaffirm her behaviour by saying, 'That's a good girl.'

Showing your approval where required is very important. For a child, the parents' approval is a reward in itself. It is a jolt for the child when loving parents express their disapproval. According to Windell, 'If you only point out how kids fall short, failure becomes a self-fulfilling prophecy.' Sincere and genuine compliments that do not sound fake to the child, should be forever ready on your lips. Ideally, if you praise or show approval to the child about three times, one disapproval is okay. If you realise that you only keep criticising the child, you need to amend this and also show approval regularly. On the other hand, if you are always praising the child, you should show disapproval or correct the child's behaviour when warranted.

Whenever a child behaves well, parents should make it a point show their approval in some way or another. It could just be a smile, a pat on the back, or a pleasant nod. Approving words like good, excellent, wonderful, or fantastic would work too. Approval should be communicated quietly, without announcing it to the rest of the family or the neighbours!

Over-praising a child should be always be avoided. For instance, it will not have the desired effect and sound fake, if a child who is being potty trained uses the potty successfully, and you clap your hands in glee and announce to all and sundry, 'Wow, how fantastic! Look everyone, how smart she is becoming! I am so proud of her!' Or, if the child wears her shoes all by herself, and you beam an exaggerated approval and exclaim, 'Wonderful! You are such a doll!' Instead, a quiet and reassuring 'Good' will work better. According to Windell, 'A praise-dependent child doesn't pursue goals for her own satisfaction. He or she may expect lavish thanks for routine chores or be unable to finish a task without more approval.' Over-praising could also embarrass or irritate children as they get older.

Parents should be consistent in showing disapproval for bad behaviour. This makes the child get used to being good most of the time. For instance, when children share their toys while playing together, you should praise them for it. If they display bad behaviour like snatching another child's or their sibling's toy, express your disapproval. If another child has a toy that your child wants to see and touch, you can gently ask the other child to show it to your child for a few minutes. The message conveyed should be that everyone should have a chance to have a good time; and that conflicts can easily be resolved between people by respecting each other's needs. By doing so, you will be explaining the reason behind such behaviour.

You should never teach your child blind obedience. If the child is told to follow orders blindly because an authoritarian figure (in this case yourself) says so, it will not hold the child in good stead in the long run. When the child grows up she will meekly follow any authoritarian voice. On the other hand, when the child understands why certain rules are in place, or why certain things need to be done in a certain manner, as a grown up, she will question things like orders from a tyrannical leader, unreasonable demands from friends, unnecessary governmental restrictions, false advertising claims etc. That is, the child will gain a useful skill for a lifetime!

It is of utmost importance that both parents should say

the same thing, consistently. So you need to talk with your spouse to make rules, and neither should break them. If parents give contradictory instructions, it is very confusing for the child. In case there are conflicting signals, the child finds it very difficult to decide which parent is correct. It causes confusion in the child and may lead to aggressive behaviour in teenage years. The child will be aware that the parent who she ignores may feel belittled, and may taunt or punish her in subtle ways. To escape this dilemma, the child may find an escape route by learning to disregard whatever either parent may say. On the other hand, the child may end up pitting the parents against each other, and make both parents fight by saying, 'But Mom/Dad said...' When children plead with one parent about changing a rule, that parent can say, 'See if you can convince Mom/Dad...,' referring to the absent parent so that children get a clear message that it is a joint decision.

Also, you should not change rules according to your mood. Suppose the child needs to complete his homework every day, the rule should not be changed simply because you happen to be in a good mood. With fixed rules in place, the child will realise that certain things need to be done in a certain manner, and there is no option on this. With this, they will also realise that there is no point in manipulating parents to change this. This kind of realisation in children will lead to greater peace in the house.

If the parents happen to have opposing views on a subject, or if they feel that they need to discuss an issue, they should always discuss it with their children. Decision-making should involve children, but making rules should be strictly debated out of the children's earshot. It could confuse children and make them insecure. Parents should always try and settle their disagreements in private. There should be no apparent disagreement between spouses on issues like finishing of homework, bedtime routine of brushing teeth, changing, and bedtime itself etc. Also, basic values should be inculcated in children by both the parents; significant things like stealing, hitting and being aggressive, or telling lies etc. are traits that are disapproved of in society. Speaking the truth is the easiest because that way, you never have to worry about remembering what you had said in the first place!

In many homes parents decide that one parent, usually the father, will pamper the child, whereas the mother will be strict and a disciplinarian. This is not good because when the disciplining parent is absent, children tend to take unfair advantage of the lenient parent.

TACKLING INDISCIPLINE

You could use a few methods to deal with disapproved behaviour, and use them consistently. Some of these are limiting TV time, or the use of the computer or telephone. Also, although it may be difficult to do, you should ignore the child's tantrums, unnecessary crying, sulking or constant quarrelling. All this will automatically stop after a while when the child realises that it fails to affect you or to get your attention.

Alternatively, to handle a tantrum or a sulk, you could say, 'Come on, you are not going to sulk, and you are a happy child. Now go to your room and come back when you are ready to smile!' Children need face saving moments, so, after a few minutes you can go to the room and bring the child out, saying, 'I knew you wouldn't sulk for long! Look at that lovely smile!'

A typical punishment we often see illustrated in the comic book *Dennis—The Menace* is Dennis being made to sit in a corner, facing the wall. This would work with a hyperactive or disruptive child. Being made to sit in a corner or in a particular room for some time would take the child away from the activity or situation that is inducing the hyperactivity, and perforce calm the child. However, a child's sense of time is different to that of an adult's. So the period for which a child is made to sit quietly in a corner or room as a punishment should roughly correspond to the child's age. For examples, four year old could be made to sit for four minutes, a five year old for five minutes, and so on. For a fiery teenager, being asked to sit quietly in a room for a few hours would work better.

Age is an important consideration when disciplining children. For a dreamy ten-year-old, clear-cut instructions are important: 'Clothes in the cupboard; school bag packed for tomorrow.'

For a preschooler, respecting other people's property and not being aggressive are the main lessons in discipline. You could ask: 'Would you like it if someone snatched your toy from you?' if the child is hankering after someone else's toys. Or, if the child is hitting you, you could just gently grab his arm and say, 'You can't hit Mom,' 'stop', 'now!' Once the unacceptable behaviour has stopped, you must try and understand what is upsetting the child. Children tend to listen when the parents are decisive.

Do not condemn children if they have done something wrong. For instance, if they forget to switch off the fan or the light, do not say, 'You are such a power-waster.' It would be far more appropriate to say, 'We must conserve power,' and switch off the fan or light yourself. This way, the child will get a clear message in a positive way, and you will not come across in a negative light either.

Teenagers can often be rude and moody, and may be prone to throwing tantrums. When such behaviour occurs, it is best to ignore it. If things are getting a tad touchy, a volcano may erupt if you try and sort things out at that very moment. However, it is important that you let it be known at that very time that you disapprove. This may be done by saying something like: 'How rude!' or 'This is bad manners,' or, 'I really don't appreciate such behaviour.' When the child is in the wrong, it is important to say so and not protect or make excuses for him.

You may bring up the subject again, after the heat of the moment has passed. You could jokingly imitate the behaviour or repeat the words of your teenager. This way you would make your point subtly. Children should be made to understand that they have to learn to control themselves, even though they may feel strongly about some issues. They need to learn that losing one's temper rarely solves a problem. In fact, people who lose their temper are most likely to feel terrible afterwards.

Bringing up children can be a trying and sometimes a harrowing experience; it is okay to lose your temper. But later, you should always admit to it, and say you are sorry about it. Parents are as human as anybody else. It is a lesson in humanism for the child to realise that. According to Schaefer: 'Saying you're sorry doesn't signal inconsistency; it signals mutual respect. It teaches kids to apologise when they're wrong, instead of digging in their heels.'

SPANKING

Spanking the child into good or preferred behaviour is the old method of handling children. However, it is not recommended any more for two reasons. For one, it is traumatic for the child to be hit. Secondly, the child will behave properly only to avoid the trauma, and will never understand why certain things should not be done. A particular kind of behaviour will be avoided in order to escape getting caught, and not because the child has internalised the need for proper behaviour. If you spank the child, it takes a second for him to fall in line. However, if you explain to the child it can take a good fifteen to twenty minutes. However, that time will be well invested, since that issue will not have to be explained/taught again.

Spanking or hitting a child may stop bad behaviour only temporarily. In the long run it backfires. Hitting can traumatise and as a result, subdue a child, causing pain and fear. Trauma can induce a child to seek revenge. It does not teach self-control, but conversely makes the child learn that it is okay for a bigger or stronger person to hit a younger one.

Instead of hitting the child, you can think up penalties in proportion to the unacceptable behaviour. Say, for example, if the homework is not done, then eating out that week could be denied. If the child misses the school bus, then she could be asked to to do some chores for you around the house, or do some outdoor tasks like going to the market or the post office, or paying some bills etc.

When children are spanked, they generally are known to continue needing to be spanked. They can also experience fear or terror in the presence of the person who spanks them. It is those children who are extroverted and externalise their problematic behaviour that are more likely to be spanked. When children are introverted, they may internalise their problems without expressing them. They may, as a result, become withdrawn, anxious or depressed. Such children, though they will escape spanking, will nevertheless carry their burden, which may eventually lead to more serious problems.

Research has shown that children who are spanked regularly, about three or more times per week, demonstrated a drop in their IQ levels. Recent research has also shown that 'corporal punishment'—hitting children to punish them—can give rise to negative traits in them like lying, cheating and a tendency towards hitting others as they grow older.

A study by Andrew Grogan-Kaylor of the University of Michigan, and Melanie D. Otis of the University of Kentucky, has revealed an amazing connection between intellectual stimulation and behaviour. Their study shows that an intellectually stimulating home environment gives children an opportunity to work through and practice their emotions, think through the consequences of their actions, and imagine possibilities for alternative actions in the future.

Andrew Grogan-Kaylor, associate professor of social work, told LiveScience.com, 'Allowing children to stretch their brains in that kind of way is allowing children to behave less anti-socially down the road.' He further says, 'To reduce the use of physical punishment, it may be beneficial to focus on interventions that teach parents to increase the amount of intellectual stimulation in the home.' Grogan's research shows that children with fewer behavioural problems come from homes with increased intellectual stimulation. The study is a result of responses from 800 respondents on questions about their use of corporal punishments, as well as many other family issues.

SELF-ESTEEM

You need to build on your children's self-esteem right through their growing years. They should be asked their opinion about issues, and should be appreciated now and again. They must be helped and encouraged in overcoming setbacks. A boost to their confidence encourages them to take responsibility. You should not keep blaming or degrading them or make them feel guilty. Watch them soar in life once you make them feel good about themselves, and give them this strong foundation. High self-esteem is the most precious legacy you can leave for your children. It is much more invaluable than a big fat bank balance or other material wealth!

We need to create an atmosphere at home that encourages children to cooperate because they care about themselves and they care about their parents. Mutually respectful communication taught at this stage will set the mould not only in the present moment, but also for the generally more turbulent adolescent years, and eventually in the adult years, when it will help them become our adult friends.

Children are not likely to always behave like angels and do what is expected and required of them. Being a parent is going to make you angry and impatient with your children on innumerable occasions. Through all these trying times, what is important is that when we speak to children we address their intelligence, their sense of responsibility and initiative, their sense of humour and their ability to be sensitive to the needs of others. We should try and avoid saying anything that would wound their spirit. We need to constantly search for a language that nourishes self-esteem.

One certain way to destroy a child's self-esteem is by being very critical of him, always telling him he is silly, or by trivialising, and thus negating any and every effort made by him. A child's self-esteem can also be shattered if he is constantly compared to a sibling or another perceived role model who apparently has very high standards. This will defeat and discourage the child even before he has had the chance to fully blossom, causing him to experience inner emptiness and pain, which will eventually stunt the child's emotional and psychological growth.

As parents, we need to provide our children with inner strength and guidance to overcome obstacles they may face in life. For inner strength to develop, personal worth needs to be ingrained in a child's personality. This can be done by encouraging children to do their best with pride and confidence. Positive self-esteem can save your children from feelings of inferiority, inadequacy and confusion.

Society recognises achievers eventually, but what about growing children? A lot of them may be potential achievers, if only provided a nurturing environment. Moreover, in order to achieve success, people need to experience a general feeling of well-being in society, which would depend, to a great extent, on a feeling of self-worth amongst its members. A child without self-worth is like a bird with its wings clipped!

A child with high self-esteem will dare to dream. He may dream of becoming a scientist or the prime minister of the country! You should always encourage it, saying things like, 'As a scientist you might become like the brilliant but absent-minded professor!', 'As a prime minister you can become really busy! What are the changes you would like to bring about?' Always encourage your child by saying something like, 'Be the best in whatever you decide to do.' Though, eventually your child may grow up to be something totally different, what is important is that he will learn to approach all situations and tasks in life with positivity and enthusiasm, and will rise to any challenges along the way with ease and fortitude.

A person with a feeling of self-worth will generally have strong convictions, and the confidence to take up responsibilities. This confidence will most likely make them succeed. Confidence will also make people with self-esteem very positive in their outlook on life, which in turn will nurture healthy and secure relationships. In a nutshell, it is more likely that people with high self-esteem will lead a more fulfilling life.

People with low self-esteem tend to be negative in their outlook. Because of their extremely poor self-image, they are surprised at compliments they may receive, and doubt their sincerity. They do not consider themselves capable, or may feel they do not measure up, so they do not take responsibility for themselves. Instead, they keep blaming everyone and everything for their failures. Disappointments pull them down a great deal, and in order to overcome them, they need to summon a great deal of strength. They love gossip and criticism because thinking of other people's frailties gives them a temporary high, and makes them feel they are not so badly off after all. They mostly feel they are very righteous and know what is best for everyone and everything. Mostly they do not have fulfilling lives. There is a danger that people around them will take undue and unreasonable advantage of them.

To tackle low self-esteem, one should set very easy goals for children. The child's self-esteem will rise with every small success. As the child's self-esteem rises, his desire to succeed and forge ahead will be kindled. A difficult task can be very daunting for a person with low self-esteem and may cause him to lose interest totally because he expects and dreads failure.

A child's confidence may be built by taking time out and patiently teaching him, for example, how to take care of and use a gadget that is mostly handled by adults, like a music system or a camera. The child will be proud to know that you can trust him with expensive and complicated gadgets. This will enhance the child's self-image in a remarkable way.

One can always work at building self-esteem by making a conscious effort to think positive about oneself, and others. You need to learn to love yourself and work hard on yourself physically and emotionally. Accepting compliments with a gracious 'thank you', learning to genuinely appreciate and compliment others, avoiding gossip and being judgemental of others, making an effort to rise with determination each time you stumble and fall, not shirking responsibility, and taking full control for your own growth are traits that will go a long way in building a positive self-image of yourself.

Changing negative self-esteem to positive requires effort, but is not impossible. However, having high self-esteem to begin with can save you a lot of effort and heartbreak. If you can give your child a sense of self worth, you are most likely giving your child a headstart on the journey of life.

There are a few simple lines from an unknown author that give simple advice on how to raise children so that they grow up to have self-esteem.

Talk with children and see that each day
each child enjoys some small successes and
some recognition as a person.

Generally while raising children, we mostly keep telling them what not to do. For instance, 'do not shout,' 'do not touch the decoration pieces,' 'do not misbehave,' etc. In the midst of all these negatives, we also need to give our children positive vibes. Indeed, parents also need to give each other positive vibes! When parents are happy and compatible, it contributes towards raising the self-esteem of children!

HOW DO YOU 'APPEAR' TO YOUR CHILD?

A child is acutely aware of the expression on a parent's face. If you greet the child with a smile and a welcoming look, she will feel wanted and loved, and as a result, confident. Likewise, a frown on your face can make a child tense.

A very good example of how your expressions and way of interacting with them can influence children was shown very well in a popular American television soap opera called *Santa Barbara*. In it, the vamp, called Gina, is shown to be a great mother to her son, Brandon. She is sympathetic to his needs, empathetic to his feelings, and always addressing and allaying his fears. She usually wears a smile on her face when she speaks with him, even though she may herself be going through tremendous stress at that time.

I remember being often asked most unexpectedly by my children why I was smiling. At those times, I was usually totally unaware of the fact that I was smiling. There were also times when I must have looked worried or frowned, since the question asked was invariably, 'What's happened?'

Children often hold a parent's chin and direct their faces to look at them, straight in the eyes, before they say what they have to. It is, therefore, important that we maintain eye-contact with children by looking at them straight in the eye. We must also make an effort to look very relaxed and at ease in their presence.

You need to make sure that in the event of a discord between you and your spouse, your children are shielded from it. Both partners should take care not to criticise nor berate each other in front of the child; instead they should always show respect and regard for each other in the child's presence. Children learn a great deal by just observing parents, so negative emotions like anger and resentment should not be displayed when children are around.

Parents should make time for themselves, independent of the time they spend with their children. This will recharge their batteries, and they will again be able to face the child with a smile. They can also utilise this time away from children to resolve issues and argue things out. It is a good idea to go for a drive with your spouse and park somewhere where you can talk without the children listening in, intentionally or otherwise!

Yes, it is tough being a parent, because you have to teach by example! Children should not be witness to negativity between parents. They should always be made to feel that they are living in a safe world, and their parents are their protective shield.

When children observe that the relationship their parents share is one of mutual respect, love and understanding, it instils confidence them. This also helps develop a loving and caring nature in them. Such children grow up to be joyful and spread cheer wherever they go! They are a delight to have around.

The feeling that they belong to a very secure family, with their parents concerned about their welfare and happiness, is very important to children. It gives them a great sense of security, so that they can then get into a relaxed state of learning in school, and a state of carefree fun on the playing field.

A child who senses an uneasy silence between her parents can suffer deep emotional distress. Unreasonable feelings of guilt may crop up in the child's mind, making her feel that she is the cause of the cold war between parents due to some reason or the other. This can cause a setback to the child's academic performance, and lead to difficulty with peers at school and even mental trauma. She can become serious, introverted, and even brood. To be happy will require a great effort on part of these children. In case parents happen to have an angry outburst in front of their children, it is important for them to apologise to each other in the children's presence, and then cool down and discuss the issue calmly in front of the child. Firstly, this makes the children relieved, and secondly, they learn that it is okay to disagree and still remain friends and live happily as a family unit, no matter what.

When a child experiences violence and anger at home, it can make the child insensitive. Since such behaviour is witnessed at home, the child does not see anything wrong with it. In fact, the child may actually imitate the same behaviour as an adult, when faced with a similar situation.

LOVE

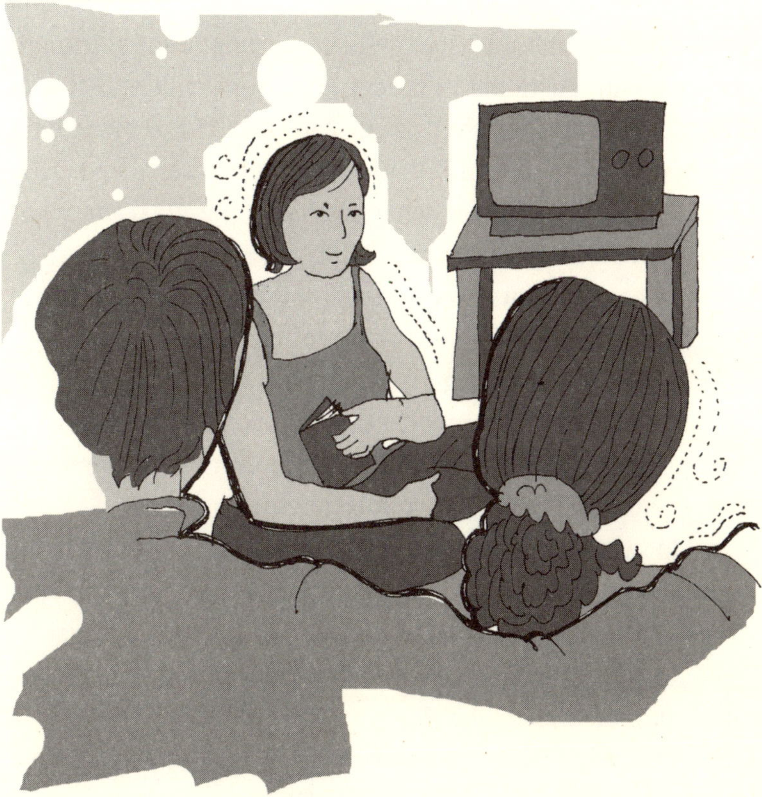

Love is a fundamental need of every child. A child can never be 'spoilt' from getting too much love. Love gives a child comfort and security, whereas a lack of it would make a child feel rejected, which could possibly make a child withdrawn, defiant or delinquent. It is not what you are giving your child materially that is important, it is your love and affection that your child experiences that is more important.

We need to give our children unconditional love, and this giving of love should never be used as emotional blackmail to justify unreasonable expectations from children. If you love your child it does not grant you the right of ownership or possession of the child. Children should receive love from their parents no matter what choices they make or what path they choose to follow in life.

It is not love, but over-protection that can 'spoil' a child. Single, or sometimes, male children may be over-protected, which can lead to negative behaviour like being fussy, demanding or being prone to throwing temper tantrums at home. Such children, used as they are to all their demands being met at home, when faced with the reality of the outside world, become bewildered and are incapable of handling the rejection of their demands and desires. This could lead them to either withdraw within themselves, or become aggressive. It may also lead to them becoming incapable of taking decisions.

When you love your children, they will be able to love their children in turn, when their time comes. That is what they have received so that is what they will know how to give. As a river flows onwards, their love will flow onward to the next generation. They may not overtly exhibit loving behaviour towards you, but they will always show you respect. It is only when they reach the age you are at now, that they will feel a sense of deep appreciation and gratitude for what you did for them. However, when their children are young, the nitty-gritty of the child rearing process will keep them pre-occupied with very little time or inclination to show gratitude to you. In the words of Gilbert K. Chesterton: 'The way to love anything is to realise that it may be lost.' Children thrive and bloom when they are loved. They can receive love from parents, grandparents, care givers, relatives, teachers—anybody. Lack of love can make children sad and lonely, making them feel neglected. Children should experience love and affection in different relationships for a more holistic view of the emotion.

Love should not be used to justify unreasonable demands on the child or to emotionally blackmail the child. Children are individuals and have the right to live their lives as they choose. Loving a child or another person does not give you possession or control of that person.

Studies now show that the lack of love in childhood and growing years is one of the root causes of evil in society. Dr Eric Fromm, in his book *The Anatomy of Human Destructiveness* has clinically examined the childhoods of fascists like Hitler and Stalin, to find a commonality. He found that their treatment in childhood had a 'high degrees of cruelty, indifference and inhuman treatment.'

Dr Fromm firmly believes it is nurture, and not nature, that is responsible for an evil-doer's mental make-up. Dr M. Scott Peck, author of the well known book *The Road Less Travelled*, believes that evil is rooted in loneliness in the childhood days.

According to the writer Lata Jagtiani: 'The best way for society to help in combating evil is to create an oasis of love and understanding at home'. Dr Kiran Bedi, the celebrated, now retired IPS officer has set up a non-governmental organisation called Navjyoti, which means 'new light.' She believes: 'Navjyoti is a sure step towards crime prevention, and has imbibed the belief in correction, crime prevention and rehabilitation with a sense of compassion and understanding.' This would effectively mean that if you could extend unconditional love to people, the chances that they will stay away from crime are very good.

According to Graham Bell in his analysis, *The Challenge of Evil*, 'When people isolate themselves from others they are unable to relate—they can only dictate. The characteristic common to all evil people is the absence of love. The evil person is incapable of giving or receiving love.'

It is only when a child experiences feeling loved, valued and protected can he feel the same for others. Children who grow with love become loving, joyful and happy adults, who are more sensitive to their surroundings and to responsibilities. Children who grow without love spend a lot of time, energy and thought looking for it. They may become insecure about it when they find it, or worse still, they may not acknowledge and accept it when it comes their way. Mentally they become so attuned to not being loved that when love comes knocking at their doors, they are likely to say a firm no.

During the first World Conference on Science and Spirituality held in New Delhi in January 2007, Dr S.C. Manchanda mentioned a very interesting experiment that demonstrated the power of love. For an experiment to assess the effect of fat on the cholesterol levels in rabbits, different batches of rabbits were given high-fat food. It was observed that this led to a rise in cholesterol levels in all except one particular batch of rabbits. On investigation, it was discovered that this batch of rabbits was fed by a young girl of twenty-two, who played with them, fondled and was generally loving towards them when she came in to feed them. It was concluded that since these rabbits received a healthy dose of love along with their fat-laden food, the offending fat did not affect them adversely!

According to Osho, love is the centre. Sex is below love and compassion is above love. Osho says: 'Very few people know what love is. Ninety-nine percent of people, unfortunately, think sexuality is love—it is not. Sexuality is very animal; it certainly has the potential of growing into love, but it is not actual love, only a potential.'

'If you have become aware and alert, and meditative, then sex can be transformed into love. And if your meditativness becomes total, absolute, love can be transformed into compassion. Sex is the seed, love is the flower, compassion is the fragrance.'

'Buddha has defined compassion as "love plus meditation." When your love is not just a desire for the other, when your love is not only a need, when your love is a sharing, when your love is not that of a beggar but an emperor, when your love is not asking for something in return but is ready only to give—to give for the sheer joy of giving—then add meditation to it and the pure fragrance is released. That is compassion; compassion is the highest phenomenon.'

According to the author and healer Louise L. Hay, if you are looking for romantic love and cannot find it, you first have to learn to love yourself! Only when you love and approve of yourself, will you attract a lover who will be bereft of need. There is nothing more attractive than a happy person. A person who is whole and complete within himself carries his own sunshine along wherever he goes! Such people are extremely attractive and difficult to resist. So, Louise Hay suggests that after you have learnt to love yourself, you should go out into the world, and have as much social interaction as possible. You should not sit cloistered at home and expect someone to land up at your doorstep, offering their love! You should strive to live a full life—doing things you want to and love to do.

INSTANT GRATIFICATION

It is important to teach children the virtue of patience. All of your children's wishes/demands should not be fulfilled immediately. Saying things like, 'We will go for ice cream once you are done with your homework,' or, 'Let us delay the holiday until we can take four days off at a time, instead of just two days now,' will teach children to plan and prioritise, and they will see the results of good planning for themselves. It will also teach them patience and self control.

When training children in this way, you need to be a hundred percent truthful and sincere. If you have cancelled a two-day holiday in February, and planned for a four-day one in April instead, you must follow it up and actually have that holiday. You must not forget about it or cancel it because something else has come up. Keeping your word will build up integrity, trust and respect in your relationship with your children.

If at times, a re-planned holiday fizzles out due to unavoidable reasons, it's all right. There is something for the children to learn in that too—provided you explain the reasons for the cancellation honestly.

Traditional values like respect for elders, or running errands for them should also be inculcated in children. Children should be made to understand that the best things in the house are for the parents. For instance, the room with the air-conditioning, the bigger room, etc. The most comfortable seat in the car or the home is to be given up for parents, when they are there, out of respect for them. The same would be applicable to other elders, like grandparents, friends of parents, etc.

Inculcating traditional values of respecting elders, and generally showing deference to them in a positive way will help children learn important things like humility, kindness and gentleness. Children should be taught to give the elderly, and people older to themselves in the household, the first choice. It could be in the most mundane of things like the choicest room or seating in the house, or other more important matters.

This may also help the child in later years during his working life, when he will be able to adjust better in an office situation where there may be a boss who demands deference. General respectfulness and humility in the office will also make him much more popular. Certain families have a restricted diet at a particular time of the year or on a particular day. These traditions too inculcate patience and self control in children. These qualities can help a child in adulthood when certain relationships do not work out, or when certain things they desire are beyond their budget.

YOUR AMBITION FOR YOUR CHILD

Many a times, parents have ambitions for their children, and these tend to be conditioned by the parents' own childhood experiences—both positive and negative. Most often, it is to do with a parent's failure to pursue a particular career of his or her liking, because of certain unavoidable factors. Say, for instance, you wanted to become a tennis player/a swimmer/an actor/a doctor, but could not, for some reason or another. Let us say that your father said, 'We can't afford tennis, we are not members of a club'; or, 'We can't afford the racquet, besides tennis balls and coaching are also expensive.' Or your parents did not do anything about your ambition to become a doctor. The parent may see this dormant desire begin fulfilled through the child, and will begin to have an unreasonable and unfair expectation from the child to choose that particular career and excel in it. The parent will be determined that come what may, the child will not be deprived of opportunities—like he or she was—and will strive to provide the child with the best possible help to achieve this end. This, in spite of the fact that the child may not at all be interested in pursuing that line, and dreams of another career.

It is important that you, as parents, do not pre-decide or pre-determine anything. Observe your child to try and identify where her interest lies, and then hone and develop that. You should nurture your child's innate talent, that is, the natural interest or talent that the child displays. If she shows an inclination towards singing, may be that is what you should encourage. If your child's forté is writing, but you push her to be a scientist, or if she wants to become a pilot and you want her to take up film-making, ultimately it is the child who will suffer. The child will not excel with ease in what she is being forced to do; but she can excel with very little effort in the field that genuinely interests her.

It will be sad if your child spends a lifetime doing something that does not interest her. This in plainspeak means parents need to let go of the ambitions that they may have for their children. This does not mean that you leave your children free and directionless to fend for themselves. You need to help your children judiciously choose and plan their careers in their field of interest. Your help and support in this area could include looking for career counsellors of repute, searching the Internet for latest developments and options in various fields, as well as financial help. Parents should remain calm and composed while discussing these matters, without getting panicky. It is important that you never belittle your child's hopes and aspirations.

LETTING YOUR CHILD BE

There is a saying in Uganda—if you plant a small tree under a big tree, you get a small tree. But if you plant a small tree next to a big tree you get a forest!

An important part of raising children is sometimes just letting them be. It is not necessary to fill every single moment of a child's time with some activity or another. It is very important to let children be free, uninhibited and spontaneous. There should ideally be designated free time in a twenty-four-hour time-frame—time in which the child is not bound by a pre-planned time-table, and can do whatever he wishes to do.

Think of yourself as a gardener, and your child as a tender sapling that needs protection, watering, nourishment and nurturing so that it can grow and bloom to its full potential. Children will blossom according to their inherent qualities, so it is essential for us to encourage them in whatever they are good at and whatever they are interested in.

According to a report by the American Academy of Paediatrics presented in Atlanta in October 2006: 'Perhaps above all, play is a simple joy that is a cherished part of childhood... . A lack of spontaneous play time can create stress for children and parents alike.'

The report further states: 'Numerous studies have shown that unstructured play has many benefits. It can help children become creative, discover their own passion, develop problem solving skills, relate to others and adjust to school settings.' Once a child discovers his passion, it is the discovery of what direction in life he will take, what will be the purpose of his actions, where he will dedicate extra time and energy. In the words of Mahatma Gandhi, 'Have a purpose—means will follow.'

Instead of being forced to watch 'get smart' videos and being exposed to activities or classes geared towards making them excel, children should be encouraged to follow regular activities and games. Simple and everyday toys like dolls and doll houses, balls and racquets or bats, or simply being around either of the parents and playing with them is much better for children. Too many hobby classes, say, dance-class, riding-class, art-class, and regular tuitions on top will be a huge burden on them.

The American Academy of Paediatrics also states in its report: 'Social pressure and marketing pitches about creating "super children" contribute to lack of playtime for many families. But so does living in low-income, violence-prone neighbourhoods, where safe places to play are scarce.'

FAILURE

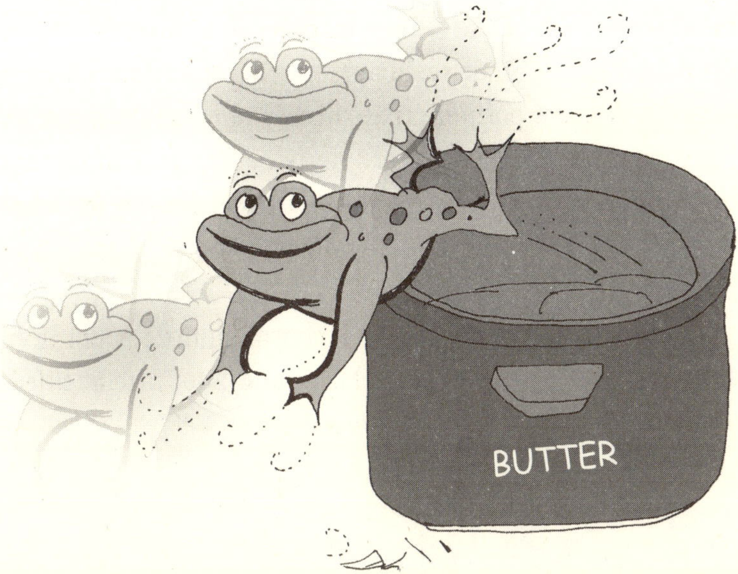
BUTTER

Winston Churchill had said, 'Success consists of going from failure to failure without loss of enthusiasm.'

Remember, it is possible—and okay—for your child to fail occasionally; it is not a matter of great shame or the end of your child's future. According to Swami Sukhabodhananda, 'Failure is the fertiliser to life.' Failure offers an extremely important lesson. It prepares children for the inevitable ups and downs of life, and is best learnt to handle in their growing years. It will help them to better comprehend and adjust to changing tides of fortune in their adult years, and teach them to take things in their stride.

There are cases of youngsters having nervous breakdowns because of heartbreak, missed career opportunities or other seemingly critical situations in their lives! It is quite possible that these youngsters may never have experienced rejection or failure before. It is important that children learn to struggle and cope, no matter what the situation, without breaking down when they encounter difficulties.

Here, I would like to quote a charming little poem from *Family Vision*, (newsletter of May–June 2000). It is titled, '*Problems!—Burdens or Blessings?*'

Two frogs fell into a can of cream,
Or so I've heard it told;
The sides of the can were shiny and steep,
The cream was deep and cold.
"Oh, what's the use?" croaked No. 1.
"We're lost, no help around!
Goodbye, my friend! Goodbye sad world!"
And weeping still he drowned.
But Number 2, of sterner stuff,
Refused to compromise
He jutted out his creamy chin
And dried his creamy eyes.
"I'll swim awhile at least," he said---
or so I've heard he said;
"It really wouldn't help this world
If one more frog were dead."
An hour or two he kicked and swam,
Not once he stopped to mutter,
But kicked and kicked and swam and kicked.
Then hopped out via butter!

MONEY MATTERS

In India, most people grow up with an incorrect perception of money. Some, who have been deprived, think too little is too much; while others, who have experienced abundance, think too much is too little. Both do not understand the true buying power of money. A good way to make your child smart with money is to give her pocket money, approximately from the age of seven, and to start with, it could be weekly.

To determine the appropriate amount of pocket money to be given, you could, for example, check out the prices of snacks available in the school canteen. You could then give the child enough pocket money to treat herself once a day, through the week. Once you have given the child pocket money, you should avoid, as far as possible, to guide her in anyway as to how she is to spend that money. The child may use it up to treat her friends or herself, and may be left without any money for the rest of the week; or she may not spend any money at all. What matters is that the child is able to make these choices independently and learns to live with the consequences. It is, therefore, important that you do not replenish the money if it finishes before the week is up. By and by, the child will learn to associate the consequences with the decisions she takes. This will be an excellent way to prepare the child to handle money judiciously later in life.

When there is balance money left over from pocket money, you may put it aside in an envelope for safe keeping.

There will be times like festivals, weddings, anniversaries birthdays etc. in the family, when the child receives money. On such occasions, do not say to the child that she is free to splurge the money and have a good time. Instead, you could ask her to buy a gift for your spouse. It could be something reasonably priced like a pen or a key chain—the idea is to teach the child sharing. The money left over would then go into the envelope, and can be used when required.

Another way to set a good example is when you receive spare change from the cashier, you put some of it into the charity boxes that most shops put up these days near cash counters (charities like Helpage India, Cancer Aid, CRY or other charities for the education of deprived children etc.). When you donate money for charity without fanfare, in a very matter of fact manner, your child will imbibe this trait just by observing you. You could then suggest, once in a while, that she donates some money to a charity of her choice.

Now, if there is Rs. 1,500 in the envelope, and the child wants to buy a bike for Rs. 2,000, you must tell her that there is a shortfall of Rs. 500. Ask what should be done to make a good the shortfall? Ask you? Save pocket money? This is to prevent the envelope from become a wish-fulfilling magic genie. The child must not learn to simply take money from the envelope for whatever she wants. Each time money from the envelope is to be taken, little sums must be done to make the child aware that the money would diminish, and she will have to start collecting it all over again to refill it.

It is also possible that the child may receive a rather large sum of money, maybe from grandparents, or from an investment. Some children may also receive large sums as pocket money. In such situations, you should put half the money in a bank and allow your child to spend the other half, Telling them that the saved amount is for their future—for their higher education, or their wedding, etc.

Handling of money should continue right through the student years. When your child is about seventeen years of age, you should hand over the envelope to her for safe keeping, or better still, encourage your child to open a savings bank account and learn to operate it.

Children should be taught how to investigate the best buys available; be it prices of onions, or air-conditioners! The concept of value for money should be discussed and encouraged. They should be made to understand that if a second hand air-conditioner is cheaper, but in bad condition, it is better to buy a new one, as that will offer better value for the money spent on it. The used one could drain the family budget by needing constant repairs. However, if the used air-conditioner is in good condition, it could be worth buying. Issues regarding money should be discussed realistically, be it the price of branded sports shoes or the family budget.

As parents, you should earnestly try and fulfil and honour all assurances and promises to your children. If you cannot fulfil a particular expectation or demand, the answer should be honest. The reason should not be one that would burden the child with the guilt for asking something from you in the first place.

Children will sometimes complain that you do not give them enough money. This happened with a friend who was bringing up her daughter as a single parent.

My friend handed over to her daughter, who was in class ten at the time, her entire salary for one month, and then asked the daughter to handle all the household expenses that month. After the month was up, the daughter realised that the money was over, while the electricity bill had not yet been paid! The daughter learnt her lesson, and never again complained of lack of money. As a matter of fact, she was motivated enough by the lesson to start earning her own pocket money!

As your child goes through her education and eventually starts earning, explain to her that she now needs to contribute a share to the running expenses of the house. Such a contribution should in fact, be expected from children as it will go a long way in teaching them their responsibilities.

You, as parents, also need to invest wisely so that there is adequate cash liquidity when the child grows up and needs money for either higher education or a wedding. There are excellent insurance policies available these days with which you can multiply your money, as it is invested and earns regular dividends. It builds a fund which you can withdraw after eighteen to twenty years, as required. This is a great gift parents or grandparents can give children. You need to ensure that premiums are paid regularly. Used positively and with care, money can afford you wonderful holidays that can expose you and your family to history and nature.

Memories of such holidays will give children strength, and a feeling of having been loved and nurtured.

If you have an abundance of money, it can be used by you and your family to create, enable, empower, replenish and thus enrich the social fabric around you.

Used negatively and carelessly, money can control or degrade other family members. Such use of money can break the backbone of the family unit. For example, if available money is used to cater to one individual's extravagant tastes and expensive interests; or if, although available, inadequate money is provided to the lady of the house to run it, and on top of it she is accused of over-spending. These are forms of exploitation to ensure control. Financial generosity should not be the pretext for making someone fall in line, pumping up someone's ego, or being overly obedient.

Money must be earned honourably, without exploiting people or the environment. Do not take huge loans you cannot repay comfortably. Pay just wages and reward the deserving. Save for a rainy day and for long term security. Children watch you closely as you deal with money, and many success stories are based on what children have observed. Recently, a non-resident Indian returned to India to start a microfinance loan system for the ordinary man on the street. He has been a great success. When asked what inspired him he said that it was the extreme poverty he observed as a child. When his grandmother was giving alms of some rice, every single grain that fell on the floor was mopped up!

DO IT YOURSELF

Children should be encouraged to do things by themselves. You can start early on this by asking your young child to tidy up after he has finished playing, and put all the toys back in the storage place. If there is domestic help, they may help, but the child should put at least half the things away all by himself.

It takes children tremendous concentration and neuro-muscular coordination to do things by themselves, both of which are very important factors in their mental and physical development. As you encourage children to do things by themselves, it is important that your spouse supports you fully. A situation should not arise that your spouse demands in front of the child that the child be left alone, and asks that the domestic help take care of things, instead of the child.

Children should be encouraged to wear their socks, shoes, vest/undergarments by themselves. While the child is making the effort, he should not be disturbed. Even if the clothes are worn incorrectly, refrain from saying anything. Praise the child for the effort when the child has finished. Then, after a few minutes, say something like, 'Hey, let me check, I think your socks are inside out,' or, 'The heel of the sock needs to be at the bottom, not the top. Just let me show you how to do it the next time.' Then proceed to show the correct way of doing it. When in a rush, dress the child yourself. Again, both parents should work together on this and support each other through it. This activity keeps the child busy too.

Never tell children to try doing things on their own, when you are in a hurry. This could make you impatient and angry. You may even shout at the child as a result of your impatience, if that happens, what lesson will the child learn? Possibly something like, 'It's better not to try,' or, 'I just can't do anything right!' Children are tender, and delicate; we can mould them any which way. We need to handle them very carefully.

Eventually, when the child can do things independently and efficiently, it is very rewarding. It gives them confidence to do other, more complex and important things in life independently and confidently when they are grown up. It also teaches them to accept failure on the path to perfection!

At this stage, when children are keen to learn, we normally stop them, and before we know it, they are 'lazy' teenagers and we then complain that they do not help out! Actually, it is we who train them not to help, in these early impressionable years.

When children receive conflicting messages from parents, it is very difficult for them to decide which parent is in the right, or which parent should be taken seriously. It causes confusion in their minds. Studies have shown that teenagers who display delinquent or aggressive behaviour are the ones who, as children, have received conflicting messages from parents. It is, therefore, imperative that both parents say the same thing to the child.

Older children should be asked to do little chores around the house, like laying or clearing the dining table, tidying their beds or dusting. A simple thank you should be said when they finish, in acknowledgement and appreciation of the effort they have put in.

Most habits are learned in the first five years of a child's life. We, therefore, have to make the most of the first few years. It requires a tremendous amount of patience, but you will reap rich dividends from the efforts you put in at this early stage in a child's life.

In the beginning, there will be a lot of bungling and messing up. Never mind; you should expect it, and be prepared for the extra effort that all the cleaning up will require. The cleanliness factor should not cause you to curb your child. When your child enthusiastically wants to serve water to a guest or be with you in the kitchen, you should happily allow it. Let him serve water in an unbreakable glass, and chat with the guest for a few minutes, and then tell them firmly that it is now time for you to spend time with your guest, and he should not interrupt. Children should be told to wish guests who are visiting, and also to say a polite 'good bye' when they leave. This will encourage social interaction.

If you are working in the kitchen, and the children want to be around, don't order them out every single time. Instead, you could give them some dough (*atta*) to play with. You could even add food colouring to the dough to make it exciting. Alternatively, give them a rusk to nibble on, or a cooking set to play with. And it's okay for boys to play with cooking sets, too!

When you are done with preparing the meal, do not instruct the child to put away his toys. Continue the play and ask what he 'cooked' for you. Sample the imaginary food that he has cooked and then ask him to eat what you have cooked for him. This would be a fun way of feeding the child. Sometimes the child may surprise you by saying, 'Can my friend also stay and eat with me?' This is because children have a great imagination. Your child may have imagined being joined by a friend when playing with the cooking set. Say 'Sure your friend can stay.' Remember your child is not possessed or crazy. Do not belittle your child or accuse him of lying about his friend. Play along and see them develop into happy, imaginative individuals who are warm and caring.

COPING WITH TRAGEDY

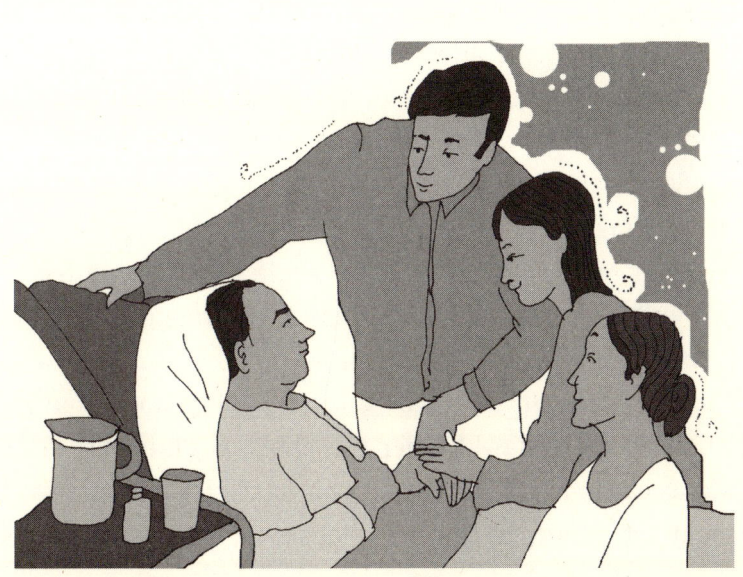

Tragedy can strike families at the most unexpected times, and in several ways. There can be events like a death, an accident, divorce, sudden loss of employment, early or forced retirement, or illness in a family. If children do not get support or direction at such times, it can cause them immense trauma. This trauma is almost certain to affect them negatively, and cause them to fall back academically, become depressed, feel guilty, and sometime, make them lose touch with reality.

When tragedy strikes the family, children should always be informed of it in precise detail—preferably by a parent or a close and trusted family member. If it is an accident, the children should be told exactly how it happened, and what the situation is. If it is an illness, then they should be explained what it means, what the prognosis is, and how they might be affected by it.

It is also extremely important to discuss their feelings with them. You should probe how they feel about the situation, and tell them what exactly you feel about it. Any feelings of guilt should be immediately negated. It is common for children, and even adults for that matter, to feel guilty and blame themselves for the emergency. There is a sad instance of a Christian woman who suddenly lost her forty-year-old daughter, and felt guilty about having gifted a black shawl to her the previous Christmas. This was because in Christian tradition, black is considered the colour of mourning. Since, if looked at sensibly, there is no way a black shawl could have caused a death, it is important to stress that such unfortunate things are a part and parcel of life, and no one can take the blame for them. The concentration should be on how to deal with the tragedy and come to terms with it. Being quiet and unapproachable will only complicate things further, and should be avoided.

Make time for and bring about situations where children can talk about how they feel. They could speak with you or any other close family member. It is also important that they know how you feel and how you are coping. If it is the death of your spouse, as one of the child's parents, you should make it clear that you too are feeling upset, hurt and are confused about how to deal with the paper-work or everyday housework. You should make it clear that you are as affected by the situation as they are, and are as traumatised as them.

If it is a divorce that you are dealing with, you must never use your children against your spouse. This particular move might affect them more adversely than the divorce itself. When one partner tries to use the emotions of the children by playing the victim in order to gain their sympathy, he or she certainly does not have the welfare of the children at heart.

In such a situation, the aim should not be to make the children hate one parent. They should be made to realise that sometimes two perfectly normal and good people find it difficult to continue living together, and therefore, decide to separate and be happy, instead of continuing to live together and be miserable. It is important for the well-being of the children that they retain love and respect for both their parents. When one or both parents set a positive tenor to the divorce, children recover faster from the setbacks it is bound to cause.

Families may face financial setbacks that result from the loss of a job, retirement, folding up of a business, or the loss of material possessions in disasters like floods or fire and so on. Children should always be actively involved in the decisions that are taken to come out of such crises, Parents should endeavour to build faith in them by saying things like, 'There is nothing that cannot be achieved with hard work,' or, 'Let's put our minds to it, I am sure we will come out with a plan on how to beat this.' In the words of the British writer James Allen, 'Circumstances do not make the man, they reveal him.'

When tragedy strikes, it is very important that you do not go into depression, or give in to self-pity and play the victim or martyr. Research has shown that teenagers are affected less by a family's economic problems than their parents' reactions to those problems. Parents are like pillars of strength to their children. With the strong backing of parents, children are able to face any challenge. Discussing with children how you all are going to manage things is healthy.

In a crisis situation, there are chances that the family may fall apart. The other possibility is that the family may mature and grow to be even closer than before. To grow and overcome a problematic situation, a family needs to plan ahead together, and to uphold its values and keep them intact. This will help them avoid taking decisions out of desperation. For instance, if the family business has collapsed, selling off assets like a factory for example, at a fraction of its actual market value will be a disaster. Or if, for example, your retirement is around the corner, it would be a bad idea to marry off your daughter in desperation to the first available person. In times of crises, you should try and maintain a calm disposition and plan things without undermining yourself or your assets. As a human being, you must hold your head high, at least out of sheer human dignity, if nothing else.

There will be times when children may feel rather lonely. You should then advice them that being alone for some length of time is not a bad thing at all. It allows time for introspection, and thus promotes self-awareness. Children should be made to understand that it is great to have friends, but if friends are not available or around for some stretches of time, this time can be spent happily in one's own company. Our happiness should never be dependent on any outside factor.

In the words of the renowned spiritual guru, Sri Sri Ravi Shankar:

Celebrate while you are alone, and
Celebrate when you are with people,
Celebrate the silence. and
Celebrate the noise,
Celebrate life, and
Celebrate death,
This is the Eleventh Commandment.

OF ROOTS AND WINGS

Giving children roots means giving them a feeling of belonging and being loved, of being rooted and grounded. With this comes a feeling of security and confidence. A sense of being related and included puts children into a relaxed state of being, and enhances observation and learning in them. Without this, there will be trauma of being lonely, and the feeling of being excluded or alienated could be very great, preventing the child from responding spontaneously and freely like other children.

How does one inculcate the feeling of belonging in children? Free and open dialogue is one way. Another way is to do things together with the children. These could be activities like gardening, playing board games like carrom or chess, or outdoor games like hide and seek, etc. You could cook with them when they are older, teaching them the basics on how to light the stove, how to tell that the water is boiling, how to heat milk, boil an egg, or make a sandwich, etc. Occasionally, you could get them to make something special for their grandparents, like a spectacle-case or a box for storing medicines. Holidaying with children, and chatting with them at leisure can be other methods of fostering a feeling of bonding and belonging.

Children should be amply encouraged to develop hobbies. Developing a hobby is therapeutic because when you work for pleasure or out of interest, a different set of brain cells are at work, which release any stress or tension that may be associated with routine. In the midst of their routine activities like studying, competing, establishing a career, an actively pursued hobby will therefore, always relax your child. Sometimes hobbies can develop into future careers, too. A hobby is a gift for life, and gives the child immense pleasure and a sense of achievement and purpose.

A psychologist lecturing at a parent teacher meeting once said that the distress caused to children in joint families, when both parents express anger, is less than in nuclear families. In nuclear families, when both parents get angry with the child, the child's world may come crashing down. In a joint family when both parents are angry with the child, and the child has the option to run to either a grandparent, aunt, uncle etc for solace, it greatly reduces the trauma or distress to the child.

Teaching the child your mother-tongue is another way of giving the child a sense of belonging. The benefits of this last the child for a lifetime. Speaking a common language in an alien environment, especially when you meet someone who belongs to the same part of the country as you do, immediately establishes a bond and a comfort level. Sharing similar rituals and festivities does the same.

Rituals are an important part of growing up. The ritual of spring cleaning the house before Diwali, laying out a rangoli, tying a rakhi on a brother on Raksha Bandhan, decorating a Christmas tree at Christmas, playing and bonding with cousins and friends, cooking together and sharing household work, and praying regularly are all roots that will give wings to your children when they grow up.

Making children interact regularly with cousins or the kids of family friends is a wonderful way of giving them friends for life. You always feel comfortable with someone you grew up with. Later, when we pass on, our children will still have roots from the past that will keep them grounded. With life's many ups and downs, friends always make the going smoother. Friends are always able to share the joys as well as sorrows of each others' lives, and as they say, a heart-to-heart with friends unfailingly refreshes the spirit.

Certain rules and rituals observed within a family also help to keep the family together. This could be the simple rule of eating or cooking dinner together. Sharing a meal is not just about eating; it is also about strengthening bonds within the family, and creating pleasant memories for the future. According to a report in the *Time* magazine, the more often families eat together, 'the less likely that kids are going to smoke, drink, do drugs or get depressed.'

Family meal times can be made interesting, and as a result, looked forward to, by perking them up with stories about forefathers and other anecdotes. Alternatively, history or geography can be discussed at the table, by sourcing information from the text or from travel books. Excellent television programmes aired on these subjects on the History Channel, National Geographic Channel, Discovery Channel, etc., can help. Sometimes, you could discuss language and its usage with, for example, idioms like, 'The reflective mind is superior to the reactive mind,' or, 'Perfection is not possible without performance of action,' etc.

You can also make it a habit to share something interesting from a book that you or someone else in the family is currently reading. This could be anything informative about other countries, people, or words of wisdom by great thinkers. This could be a great way of honing one's language skills. A dictionary can be kept at hand to look up meanings of words that are difficult to understand. You could also just sit with an atlas and look up locations of various counties or cities.

One bad practice that the family as a whole must give up is the habit of having TV dinners. This is a habit that induces lethargy, cuts communication, and impinges on personal time.

Also, it should not be your sole responsibility to make dinner time interesting. Everyone should be encouraged to share something interesting. Be it a joke, an anecdote, an article, even an account of the day's happenings. Dinner time should not be used to check with each other whether chores or homework have been completed. It should be a pleasant experience for everyone. Speaking on the phone at meal times should be another strict no-no. Thus, sharing a meal together with the family makes the children learn several important social skills, the art of good conversation, the art of listening to others, and the habit of acknowledging different points of view.

A recent study by Columbia University on families eating together shows that children who mostly eat with their parents are forty percent more likely to say they mainly get As and Bs in school, than children who have upto two family dinners per week. The study further reveals that family dinners get better with practice, 'the less often a family eats together, the worse the experience is likely to be.'

Eating together also promotes a sense of belonging and security in children. According to M. Weinstein, 'We've sold ourselves on the idea that teenagers are obviously sick of their families and that they're bonded into their peer group. But we've taken it to an extreme. We've taken it to mean that a teenager has no need for his family. And that's just not true.'

However trivial and inconsequential the above mentioned activities seem to be, their importance is invaluable. This fact is illustrated by a newspaper report published on 11 November 2006. It said that for the first time in sixty years, Nazi baby-farm children (i.e. children who were intended to be the foundation of Hitler's proposed Aryan 'master race') from the 'Lebensborn programme' met in Wernigerode, in East Germany. These children were born through a special programme, from SS soldiers and blond, blue-eyed women, in camps across Europe. They were taken from their mothers at birth and given to adoptive parents, to be brought up under a strict Nazi regime. Although Hitler and his SS chief might have thought they were creating a superior race, according to Matthias Meissner, 'To this day, many of them suffer from the consequences of secrecy and the Nazi ideologies of race. The lack of affection and poor education, besides Nazi indoctrination, has led many of them to become adults who are educationally backward and emotionally crippled.'

It is, therefore, no wonder that Mother Teresa said that the hunger for love is greater than the hunger for bread. According to the spiritual guide, T.L. Vaswani in his book *Breakfast with God*: 'The deepest pain arises not from hunger, nor cold, nor illness, nor imprisonment.

'The deepest pain arises from within the soul! Yes, the deepest suffering is not physical, but spiritual.'

FOOD HABITS

Nutrition is most crucial during the first five years of a child's life, and particularly so in the first three years. It may be said that the foundation of an individual's health is laid during this period. While a new born baby should ideally be exclusively breastfed during the first six months of its life as this provides children with all their nutritional needs in perfect balance, it is also absolutely necessary to start with complementary feeding at six months, along with breastfeeding.

A baby's brain development depends on three factors—genetic, nutritional and environmental (emotional). Breastfeeding takes care of two of these, i.e., nutritional and environmental. It thus provides the very significant emotional factor to the baby.

There is evidence to suggest that breastfed babies are less likely to suffer from allergic disorders (mainly of the skin and respiratory type), dental caries, obesity, high blood-pressure, heart disease etc. in later life. In order to have adequate and nourishing breast milk, the mother needs to have nourishing food and eat at least twenty-five percent extra as compared to her pre-pregnancy food intake. She should also drink plenty of liquids to replenish fluids lost through breast milk.

The good thing about breastfeeding is that it encourages weight loss in the mother!

The baby takes away about 120 calories per kilo of its body weight, through breast milk. So, a newborn weighing

3 kilos will take away 360 calories, plus about 40 calories more. As the baby grows and gains weight, it uses up an increasing number of calories. Also, if the mother feeds only from either one of the breasts during a feed, the baby consumes the end milk in the mother's breast, which is very high in fat content. This makes the mother lose weight and helps the baby gain weight! It has been further proved that a mother who breastfeeds her baby is less likely to get cancer or osteoporosis in later years.

Complementary feed starting at the age of six months helps to prevent faltering growth and malnutrition, which normally occur during this stage. After six months, the baby should be fed staple foods that the family has, for example, kheer, halwa, upma, curd, etc.

Food from packets and jars should be avoided as far as possible. Such food contains preservatives, and is stale, for all intents and purposes. There will be ample exposure to preservatives, chemicals and pollution in general in the baby's later years, so it's a good idea to minimise the consumption of preservatives at this stage.

Baby foods available in the market are also exceptionally smooth textured and are often made out of raw cereal. There is a strong possibility that babies will get accustomed to the smooth texture, and later reject regular home cooked foods. If babies do not eat a variety of food, as it is made at home, it can become deficient in essential micro-nutrients. Also, smooth raw cereals could get lodged in the folds of the baby's intestines, and giving rise to unexplained stomach pain years later, as this cereal putrifies in the gut.

In general, a one year old child requires half the amount of food the mother requires. However, since children have a small stomach, they need small but frequent meals. Porridge or oats can be the first complementary food that an infant has. The addition of oil or fat to these provides additional calories required by the baby. Gradually, foods made from a cereal and pulse mixture (e.g. khichdi or idlis), green and yellow vegetables, and also fruit should be introduced into the diet.

Introduction of new foods should be done at the rate of one new food per week. So, if it is oats one week, it can be bananas the next week, and may be porridge the following week. This way, if the baby ever reacts with an allergy to a particular food, you will immediately be able to pin-point the offending food. It would be a good idea to try new food on a Monday, Tuesday or any other working day, so that you can reach a doctor easily if required.

A normal family diet should be suitably modified to suit the needs of infants. Some good options are boiled mashed potatoes, or over-cooked, soft khichdi. Alternately, it could be chappati mashed in hot dal with a little ghee. The chappati should be allowed to soak and blend with the dal. These foods will help meet the baby's requirement of additional calories and micronutrients, while breastfeeding will ensures the supply of good quality proteins essential for growth.

The daily frequency of feeding an infant with foods other than breast milk, should be as detailed below:

At 6 to 8 months: 2 to 3 times a day.

At 9 to 12 months: 3 to 4 times a day.

At 12 to 24 months: combined with additional nutritious snacks, 1 to 2 times a day.

When feeding these complementary foods, the child should be made to sit in a high chair at the dining table and fed at the time adults are eating. This will give the child the thrill of eating with grown-ups, and you won't have a problem in feeding him, since kids love to imitate adult behaviour!

Around the age of a year and a half, your child may suddenly want to eat all by himself. Initially, while attempting to direct the spoon to his mouth, the child may direct it to his cheeks or ears instead, and spill half the food in the process! Slowly, the child's co-ordination develops and improves, he will learn to aim the spoon directly at the mouth. But a period of trial and error is inevitable. At such times, a little tussle may ensue between the parents and the child, as they try and hold the child's hands down while they attempt to stuff the food in his mouth. Sometimes, the parents will switch on the TV so that as the child's attention is drawn away from the act of eating, and while he watches TV, they shovel food into his mouth! Depending on the child's interest in the TV programme, he will either over-eat or under-eat. So, TV viewing and story-telling is not recommended when feeding children.

When the child is eating, his concentration should be entirely on the food. Distractions when eating affect digestion. As a child looks at the food, observes its colour, texture, and concentrates on its flavour, the body releases saliva and other digestive juices, aiding digestion. Inadequate release of digestive juices can cause gas, heartburn and other digestive disorders.

Self-feeding by children can lead to a big mess. Children drop food, experiment and play with it, but learn as they do so. They drop food since they cannot aim right, or because they want to experiment, say, by dropping water and seeing it splash and spill, and then drop a piece of bread and see it just plonk on the floor without spilling or bouncing. They may squish rice in their fists to feel its texture. They may try to grab handfuls of water and other liquids, and learn that they can't. They might experiment with different food combinations to check out the variation in taste, for example, adding water to rice, and learn that the combinations that you give them are generally far tastier.

So while children eat, they also learn through experimentation. Parents should be prepared for it. For this reason, carpeting in your dining area is inadvisable. Organising extra help for cleaning up is also a good idea, as the baby may need to be sponged and changed after a meal. Your reward will come after about six months, when the child will eat the food put in front of him like an angel, without making a mess! All the coordination and experimentation will then be behind you. It is important to allow this phase as it will also teach the child to 'handle' food. Many school-going children who have not gone through this phase may not eat food from their lunch boxes at school, since they do not like to mess their hands! They are simply not geared to handle food.

Today, children are becoming more obese and spend a lot of time sitting rather than running and playing around. They have to learn to stop eating when they are full. Therefore, parents should not insist that they finish all the food on their plate. The old rule of 'Finish everything on your plate' is quite obsolete today. Mealtimes should be pleasant and should be provided at regular intervals, with a good variety of foods.

Children should not be disciplined or reprimanded at the dining table. Small children, like restless toddlers, should sit for at least fifteen minutes at a stretch at the dining table, so that they have enough time to eat the required amount of food. You should try and avoid instructing children on what dish they should taste, and which they must avoid. Children who are allowed to eat spontaneously, as they please, are less likely to over-eat and have all varieties of foods.

It is recommended to serve a variety of foods—protein, carbohydrates, vegetables, bread, fruit and milk. Ellyn Satter, author of *Secrets of Feeding a Healthy Family* recommends, 'Pair familiar with unfamiliar food, favourite with not-so-favourite. Sooner or later, kids will learn to like most things.' You can generally restrict foods like candy, fizzy drinks and other junk food, but indulgence should be allowed once in a while. There should be no hard and fast rule regarding this. According to Wurtman and Marquis in their book *The Good Mood Diet*, 'Carbohydrates are as essential for weight loss as petrol is to a car. They not only drive the system that controls appetite, they also control emotional eating and mood.'

A study of girls aged between five to seven years in the year 2002, published in *The American Journal of Clinical Nutrition* showed that girls whose access to snacks was restricted, were more likely to gorge on food than their peers. If children are hungry between meals, a biscuit, some savouries or candy will not harm them.

If you are worried that your child is not eating enough, always check with your doctor. If the child's growth is consistent, chances are he is fine.

PLAY

Children earlier grew up climbing trees, kicking ball, scraping their knees and elbows, running around barefoot, playing with neighbourhood children of all ages. Children today are exposed to television since birth, and can sit for hours playing computer or video games. They wear designer clothes and have fairly busy, independent, social lives. They hardly know their neighbours and their busy schedule leaves them with very little free time.

One does not need to spend money for an infant to enjoy play. A baby will be equally happy with a bowl and spoon to create a din, instead of a rattle, or nibbling at a humble rusk, instead of an expensive teething ring.

TOYS

There are electronic toys available in the market for children. For instance, there is a toy that has a ladder and a fireman, in which the fireman starts to climb up and get down the ladder at the press of a button. After working it repeatedly, a child is eventually bound to get bored of a repetitive toy of this kind. Children need toys that encourage their imagination and creativity, rather than toys that offer passive entertainment.

Toys should be safe and environmentally friendly. A simple set of wooden blocks can make a great toy. It can be piled-up like a tower and then knocked down; it can be made into a runway for dinky planes, a parking lot for dinky cars or a doll house for a doll.

Children can play with just about anything, ranging from empty match boxes, shoe boxes, medicine bottles and marbles, sand, mud, beetles, flowers and leaves, etc.

It is important to check toys for safety. For instance, a baby should not be given a marble, which may be swallowed and will choke the baby. Similarly, stuffed toys that have easily detachable additions like a buttons and beads that can be swallowed, and plastic bags that can be pulled over the face, thus choking a child, are potentially dangerous. For older children, toys that may break easily with a little rough handling should be avoided.

TOY TIPS

Children have short memories. You can put away some of their toys in storage and pull them out after a few months, to 'add variety.' Rotation of toys will mean more variety and more enjoyment for the child

Toys do not necessarily have to be washed with an antiseptic solution. Washing with soap and water, and sun-drying them for at least thirty minutes is as effective. Half an hour of strong sunshine acts as a great disinfectant!

Batteries should always be removed when storing electronic toys. If left in place, they can leak and damage the toy.

The child's preference should be the only criterion when choosing a toy. Some parents maybe nostalgic about toys or books they longed for or loved as children, and this might compel them to force their choice on their children.

A toy that is too complicated for a child of a certain age can be put away, and brought out when the child is ready for it.

AGE ZERO TO ONE

In the beginning, a baby simply likes to watch other children play. For a baby below the age of one year, play means grabbing interesting objects and sucking at them, thumping them or throwing them around. Below and around the age of one, children like to play peek-a-boo, and clapping and whistling games. They also enjoy traditional baby rhymes accompanied with rocking, moving or swinging motions. Riding piggy-back on someone is also something that they enjoy immensely.

When babies begin basic interaction, they start grabbing toys from other children and crying or fighting over them.

AGE ONE TO THREE YEARS

As children pass the age of one year, they might like to play alongside other children. Some years later, as pre-schoolers they like to play with clay, paper and crayons, coloured wooden beads etc. They can be taught how to make shapes like balls, squares, birds, trees and so on with dough. They can also be taught to draw basic shapes and figures like aeroplanes, houses, trees, clouds, the sun, a mouse etc. with crayons. Different coloured wooden beads can be strung with rope in batches of five to teach them how to count. They can be given used envelopes to colour and paste together making long buntings, which can be used to decorate the home on birthdays.

There are many ways to keep smaller children happily

occupied around the house. They can be asked to fill the clothes basket with freshly dried clothes, or empty a carton of toys, and re-fill it neatly. They can have fun trying to fold clothes, or neatly stack folded clothes. They can help laying spoons on the table. Children at this age play willingly with anyone available. While doing these things the mother can teach the child counting or the alphabet, by singing it out. The child can be taught counting while arranging spoons or stacking socks. This will teach the child household responsibilities and participation, a valuable habit they will carry over into adulthood. After a little guidance, the children should be left to play independently and adults should refrain from too much interference, which can erode the child's interest in play.

AGE THREE TO SIX

Three to six year olds love to imitate adults. They might imitate movie stars, role models or their parents. Girls might wear their mother's clothes and sandals, and may mother their dolls. Boys could also enjoy playing with dolls or miniature cooking sets. Children may imitate having an intense conversation, complete with mannerisms and style of an adult of their choice—their father, uncle or maybe a film-star.

When children are about five to six years old, parents in the same locality or building can organise daily play-groups in each other's homes, at a mutually convenient time.

Children in this age group also could get destructive, and break toys and maybe things around the house, too. Good buys for children at this age would be tricycles or bicycles, a football, blocks, dolls, dinky cars, etc. It is also important to expose children to books, which should start at the earliest possible, maybe at one year or less. The ideal books for children would be  books depicting different colours or shapes, with pictures of familiar objects like houses, trees, dogs, birds, and books with simple stories for children, books about numbers and counting, about opposites, time, air, water etc. There are books available in which children can paste matching stickers of shapes, animals or objects in relevant places; easy jigsaw puzzles, like the large sized wooden ones that have pictures of birds, shapes or trees in large size cut-outs that children will find easy and interesting to realign in the puzzle.

For older children from about eight years of age, books with the *Panchtantra* stories, the *Jataka* tales, and the wonderfully illustrated and very informative *Amar Chitra*

Katha series are highly recommended. These provide a basic understanding of our culture and tradition, as well as introduce children to our mythical and folk heroes and historical figures. This is especially significant in today's world, where there are no grandparents at home any longer, who will introduce children to this kind of valuable learning.

Children at this age like to play until they are tired, when they like to either fall asleep, watch television or be read to. They also become choosy as to whom they would like to play with. They start forming friendships and identifying with a particular group of friends.

AGE SEVEN TO TWELVE

At the age of seven to eight years, children start enjoying playing in groups or teams. They are likely to enjoy board games played in large groups. Just a generation ago, children of this age enjoyed playing games like cops & robbers, seven tiles or *pithu*, hide and seek etc. At this age, today's children are more likely to get seriously involved with video games.

Children can also start to swim, play basketball, badminton, tennis, football or any other game that is available at school or outside. They may also enjoy indoor games like cards, ludo, snakes and ladders, carom, puzzles, monopoly etc. These games will probably be enjoyed when it is too hot or cold to play outside, or there is lack of playing space available in the open, on holidays and when recovering from an illness.

TEENAGE

As children grow older and enter puberty, their interest in games requiring active participation may decline, and they may switch from video games to reading, music, sports, gyming etc. As children grow into adolescents, special equipments like racquets, balls and other sports gear etc, may be required, in order to participate in active sport. Also, special facilities like playing fields, club or gym memberships, transport and so on will be required. It is therefore, more likely that such activities are limited to the higher socio-economic groups. Other children may lack time due to household duties, studies and lack of encouragement from parents.

SIGNIFICANCE OF PLAY

Play is particularly important for children as it encourages social adjustment. While playing with other children of their age, they learn how to establish social relationships and how to solve the problems that arise with these relationships.

Children of the same age may vary in their capacity to play certain games. One should accept each child's individual pace of development in play. It is important that adults do not play very often with children. Adults tend to allow children to win, so when a child loses when playing with another child his own age, he might not be able to handle it, and might throw a tantrum. Playing with adults gives a child unrealistic ideas of his ability, whereas playing with other children gives a child a true insight into his abilities and helps create a definite, realistic, concept of self.

A child also learns to accept what is considered right and wrong by the group he is playing with. He learns to accept rules, be cooperative, truthful and a good sport. These traits carry over into adulthood and help form a pleasing personality.

Play also helps children to develop the muscles in their body and provides an outlet for surplus energy. When energy is not exhausted in play, it can make children tense, nervous and irritable. Play also encourages communication skills, so that children learn to understand what others are saying, and to express themselves in a manner that will be understood.

Play also provides an invaluable outlet to children's emotions or desires. A child who has been scolded, will scold her doll in turn and feel better. A child who is otherwise too timid to be a leader, will enjoy commanding and leading his toy soldiers.

TOO MUCH, TOO LITTLE AND SOLITARY PLAY

It is important that children be taught to balance play and work activities so that they imbibe a good sense of personal and social adjustment. Many a times, parents unnecessarily allow children extra time to play. This is often done at the cost of study time and the time spent in learning to do regular household chores like tidying one's room or cupboard, clearing the table or taking on some other responsibilities around the house.

Play should neither be excessive nor completely absent. Too much play becomes repetitive and monotonous for a child. Children need to keep changing their activities in order to remain interested and refreshed. Too much dedicated play time can easily bore children. Boredom leads to lethargy, so that they are bound to expend lesser effort in doing things they are capable of. Consequently, they will not put

in their optimum effort, and their achievement levels will be much below their capability.

When children become under achievers, they begin to lack the desire for taking initiative, and as a result miss out on appreciation and recognition from teachers, parents and people in general. Social recognition is important for children in order to have a positive image of themselves in their minds.

Further, children generally develop a negative attitude towards 'work'. Having never done it before, they may even lack the confidence to do it. They may start thinking of work as something that should be avoided as much as possible because it is an unpleasant activity. This might lead to the development of a general anti-work attitude, or a habit of procrastination in their personality. This may well harm the child's personal and social adjustment skills in adult life. Hence, too much play, like too little play, is a sign of social maladjustment.

Some children may avoid active social interplay and may concentrate on playing all by themselves. The reasons for this may be lack of space, traffic hazards outside the house, parental encouragement to play by themselves, lack of children of the same age around their home etc. Solitary play is also important as it can develop into a hobby as a child grows older. It can also help the child overcome a period of illness or convalescence, or adjusting after moving to a new area where he initially doesn't have friends. Also, at a particular age, children enjoy solitary play—things like reading or listening to music. This can help provide identification with friends, since children often get together and discuss music or books, and thus feel part of 'the gang'.

Single children or lonely children may enjoy having a pet of their own, to love and care for. Looking after a pet is known to reduce stress and blood pressure in adults. It also provides the child with someone to play with, who also gives them unconditional love! This makes children feel good and teaches them about loving and caring. Since animals have a shorter life span than humans, the eventual loss of a pet will teach children how to deal with loss.

Pottering about in the garden is a very soothing activity. Gardening could be developed into a very satisfying hobby. It is not only refreshing to be with nature, it also puts children in touch with the weather and seasons etc., and teach them the rhythms of nature. Weeding the lawn, planting seeds, tending to a kitchen garden, eating home-grown fruit and vegetables can be very satisfying to a child.

However, children who indulge in too much solitary play may end up thinking of themselves as 'loners', 'different' or 'inferior' because that is the way other children their age may regard them. It is important that a balance be struck between active play and solitary play, and between play and work.

TV, INTERNET, GAMING

The television constantly competes for the attention of children. As the TV is switched on, cartoons, wars, news in all its graphic detail, music, movies and so on can enter a home and pervade the atmosphere. It is important to be selective with this information overload. It is time consuming, but extremely important for parents to check out programmes before letting children watch them.

A case in point is cartoons. It may seem that it is safe to allow children to watch cartoons. However, recently a cartoon programme on a particular cartoon channel earned the displeasure of many parents and psychologists alike. A newspaper article (*The Times of India*, 18 January 2007) reported: 'Shin Chan (a five year old) often makes life miserable for his homemaker mother. He disturbs her when she tries to take an afternoon nap. He makes fun of her weight consciousness. He calls her "*bacche churane wali moti budhiya*" (an old woman who steals children), though she neither is old or fat and of course she does not steal children.

TV viewing needs to be restricted and a balance struck between watching television, school work and home duties. Television becomes a major hazard when parents put children before it when they themselves are too tired to be bothered or simply want to be left alone. At such times, parents do not care to check what the children are viewing.

It is important that parents interpret what children see

on the screen. For instance, in Hindi movies, the hero and heroine are shown performing dance movements that are nothing short of gymnastics. A normal person could easily pull a muscle trying out such movements. Many TV soaps show scheming and plotting and murky politics in homes. This kind of audacious behaviour is far from reality, and totally undesirable. These may plant strange and negative ideas in the innocent and naïve minds of children.

Excessive violence should be criticised as socially disapproved behaviour, and viewing of programmes depicting it should be kept to the minimum. Watching too much violence, torture and cruelty on screen desensitises children, i.e., it takes away their sensitivity. They may start to perceive delivering punches, blows and firing of guns as normal behaviour, and fail to see the damage caused by such physical attacks. They may consider violent behaviour as usual, and accept it more readily as normal behaviour in real life in their adulthood, too.

It is important that empathy be nurtured in children so that they grow up to understand and regard others' perspective with respect. This helps them grow into more helpful and understanding adults and, as a result, more balanced individuals. Parents can, for example, tell a toddler, 'It hurts me when you pull at my hair. If you keep doing it, I wouldn't want to be near you.'

According to Michael Chandler of the University of Rochester, 'A child's anti-social behaviour may stem from his inability to see the world from anyone's point of view but his own.'

Children should be made aware that unrealistic situations so often portrayed on television are far removed from reality. Characters are stereotyped in movies. For instance, villains may not be shown to have an iota of goodness in their character. Mothers are always good, fair and perfect. People of a particular community or profession may be portrayed in typical stereotype. The hero is perfect in looks, compassion, integrity etc. All these stereotypes can influence a child's attitude towards people and reality. Movies can typify people and not touch upon the in-between over-lapping areas of people's personalities.

Besides, glamour attracts children, and most movies show villains as having a wonderful time and gaining attention through antisocial acts. As opposed to this, the hero may be shown as struggling. Children may be more attracted to villains due to the glamour, feeling of power and comfort that they exude, and may identify with them and use them as role models to fashion their own personality.

What escapes children is that antisocial behaviour does not pay. A bully, for instance, may get to use a swing more often, but will eventually be left friendless and alone. Illegal manoeuvers will bring with them instant rewards, but lead to tensions or fear of being nabbed.

Besides, children may be glued to the TV set and communication within the family may suffer, since, while watching TV, a child will not like to converse or do things with the family. It might also upset the child's study, sleep and meal time schedules. Depending on programmes watched, a child's pronunciation or use of language, can be affected. TV can also keep children away from outdoor activity, fresh air, physical exercise and interaction with their peer group.

If children always watch programmes with happy endings, they expect everything in their lives to also turn out right. This could give rise to unrealistic expectations. If this does not happen in their personal lives, they might imagine they are being discriminated against, maybe by a particular group of people and being made martyrs of. It is, therefore, important to protect children from false or glamourised concepts of what the world is all about. TV watching should be limited to a particular time, and particular programmes should be selected for viewing. Never place a TV in the child's room. The child may watch undesirable programmes late into the night, and, consequently, be unable to get up in the morning, may fake a headache or stomachache in order to miss school.

In today's boom of satellite television, we must make an extra effort to keep control on TV watching and keep our children in touch with reality, so that their social and personal adjustments in life are well balanced.

The journal of the American Academy of Pediatrics, called *Pediatrics*, published a study by Kamila Mistry that says: 'A number of studies have demonstrated negative effects of heavy television viewing. However, timing of exposure is an important consideration. Reducing viewing to acceptable levels can reduce risk of behavioural and social problems.' The pediatrician's group has issued guidelines that discourage television viewing among children younger than two years, and recommended children older than two limit their viewing to less than two hours daily. The group also recommended against having a television in a child's bedroom. 'Despite these recommendations, many young children are consuming significantly more than two hours of television', the report mentioned.

THE INTERNET

The internet is truly an amazing new revolution of our times. It has brought communication and any information in the world you wish to have to your desk and your mobile phone at the tap of a few keys, wherever you may be in the world! It is a very powerful tool, and like all powerful tools, it needs to be used with utmost skill and discretion. It can be used with equal ease for research, or for gaining sinister knowledge on how to make bombs; it can be used to communicate with family or for communication between criminals.

It is like an electric saw, which if used to chop up the furniture in the house can cause senseless destruction. However, if used discriminately it can be of immense use to carpenters and builders.

The internet can be used to get information for homework, or, conversely to visit pornographic sites. Everything on the net may not be the truth. People often morph photos and portray lies on the internet about themselves or others.

The information you get on the internet, if not from an authentic source, may be incorrect.

There are also chat rooms one can enter on the internet to talk to others netizens, people you may have never met. When you enter a chat room, both you and the person you are 'chatting' with fill out detailed descriptions of your selves, as an introduction. There have been many cases where perverse adults have impersonated their true identity to befriend children and have often ended up sexually exploiting them.

A blog is a personal site anyone can create on the internet. It is a random site and has no format. A blog can be like someone's personal daily diary; or a site on which you can share ideas on any subject, be it thoughts of teenagers, thoughts on political ideologies, cooking, art, etc.—just about anything. You can start a blog on any subject that interests you. Some blogs on the internet are full of hate messages, or perverse ideologies.

So, there are many negatives to the internet, apart from the information advantage. Children can be protected from the disadvantages of internet by giving them limited access to it.

Corporate houses, service provides, authors, individuals, charities, educational institutions and so on can create their own web-sites, which can be accessed through the internet. These web-sites give detailed information on whatever the company represents. Some web-sites are interactive, that is, you post questions on them that can be answered.

Usually you can download admission forms of educational institutions from the internet. You can also buy things off the internet, be it books, railway or airline tickets, holiday packages, clothes, medicines, health and fitness equipment, etc. There are various payment options available to pay for what you buy on the internet. You can pay all your electricity and phone bills on the internet. Given all the myriad features of the internet, a child definitely needs to be familiar with it and its working.

VIDEO, COMPUTER GAMES

Video games are said to enhance neuro-muscular coordination. That is, the time taken for a person to respond physically to his/her thoughts is faster and more efficient as a result of playing video games. It is also said that it results in weight reduction, since, as people play, they get totally engrossed and forget to eat! Conversely, it is said to make people gain weight, since they are always sitting and gaming, and do not move about enough! Some experts believe that action video games are good for eyes. Innumerable conflicting claims have been made in connection to the merits and demerits of video games, and these are likely to multiply.

What is important to remember is that to be constantly staring at a video game screen or the TV, is likely to create eye strain. It is, therefore, recommended that while gaming continuously, occasionally one should look away from it at the farthest point possible. It could be a glance at distant tree-tops or a patch of sky; or looking out of the window to see the traffic or the city skyline. Alternatively, one could shut one's eyes and gently cover them with two fingers, or rub the eyelids gently with two fingers.

In January 2007, an article in *The Times of India* reported that a child becoming addicted to video games has become very common in the city of Mumbai. Every metro city in India, for that matter, has children getting hooked on to these games. These games are mostly full of violence.

There are usually games where aliens are out to destroy humanity, warriors out to destroy the dark forces, demons, monsters, and war scenarios etc. There are fights and gun battles, murder, selection/buying and selling of weapons/ammunition, etc. Some games propose make you get re-energised when you suck someone's blood, while some give you extra lives when you kill! According to child psychologist Hemangi Dhavale, 'When children are regularly exposed to electronic violence they begin to consider violence as completely normal even in everyday life.' (*The Times of India*, 29 June 2005).

According to Shyama Chona, former principal of Delhi Public School, R.K. Puram, New Delhi, 'Children are becoming impatient and intolerant these days. Violent games are affecting their behavioural patterns and language. With parents not being able to spend adequate time with their kids, they tend to compensate by providing them with such computer games. However, we have been conducting special orientation programmes for parents to encourage kids to play traditional games.' (*The Times of India*, 2 October 2007).

Multimedia game manufacturers are partnering with Confederation of Indian Industries (CII) to develop games based on mythology, sports and education. 'In games like Age of Empire and Rise of Nation, players are given a choice to discover the Indian civilisation right from Stone Age to modern era. 'Similarly, we will be launching another set of video games, where students from class III to XII can learn their lessons in math, science and social studies, play quiz with their friends and test their knowledge skills,' says M. Anand, Country Manager, Microsoft Entertainment and Devices Division.

'A set of educational games like Bookworm, Diner Dash and Professor Fiz test the children's expertise on spelling and writing skills. We have been pursuing the CII to promote a platform of e-sports to encourage kids play these games and compete with each other at national and international levels,' says V. Gondal, founder of India Games Pvt Ltd.

Some games also have cartoon characters like Scooby-do the dog, or characters from Disney world, like Donald Duck, for instance. When playing the game one can win points in accordance to the number of hurdles overcome; or the number of killings accomplished. Money can also be won on the game. One game can be played by many people.

A study in Germany was conducted on eighteen to twenty-six year olds, as they played their video games. Magnetic Resonance Imaging (MRI) showed that as these games were played, a part of the brain that makes you feel emotions, particularly the emotion of empathy went numb, while the dorsal part of the brain associated with aggression became hyperactive. In Russia in 2005, a twelve year old boy died of brain haemorrhage after spending hours on video games.

The director of Indian Institute of Technology (IIT), Chennai is rumoured to have said that he was less bothered about porn than game addictions. IIT Chennai turns off its server from 1 am to 4 am so that students stop their e-games. Although the games provide fun and entertainment to students, and make them feel powerful and in control, many find that their grades drop as their addiction to the games gets stronger. In an extreme case, a student of IIT Powai, in Mumbai, who was an obsessive gamer, committed suicide.

Doctors say that the games sap children's mental energy, causing fatigue. According to child psychiatrist Nirmala Rao, 'Such games increase the pressure on children's brains, leading to increased aggression and a lower frustration threshold.' This is probably why a little boy, addicted to video games, shows occasional aggression by kicking and punching passers-by. His mother says, 'I am aware of the negative effects and so have started restricting the time he spends at his play-station.'

Gaming, however, is getting increasingly popular as software multinationals target the Indian market. Also, in-game advertisers have taken to embedding their product advertisements deep into the game's software codes. Games are, therefore, here to stay and are likely to be marketed aggressively. It is parents who need to make sure that it does not become an obsessive compulsion with their children. One way to do it is to limit the time children spend on playing these games. They can also find out which games are less violent, and get those for their children instead of the more violent ones.

Children can spend hours all by themselves watching TV, playing computer games or being connected to the internet. The more time they spend in this manner, the less time they will spend with family and friends. It interferes with their ability to socialise. This lack of socialising skills makes it difficult for them to get along with others in the work place or in other social situations later in life.

Today several children spend about twenty to thirty minutes playing video games daily and spend about two to three hours daily watching TV. When children meet they often play video games together, or they play video games with parents, siblings or grandparents. Card games like "Patience", board games like "Scrabble", ball games and other sports can all be played on the computer today. Even books can be read as e-books on the computer. Spellings can be checked easily on spell check.

Sitting in front of the computer or TV or playing a video game requires one to be in a stationary position over long periods of time. The only movement or physical activity involved is that of clicking the remote control or the computer mouse. One could be sitting like this for hours.

On the other hand, alternative activities like dancing, playing a musical instrument, walking in a park, birdwatching, gardening, playing with other children, helping in the kitchen or with house work, etc. should be encouraged. Children need to be close to nature; they need to be physically active and working different muscles in their body.

It is fun for children to grow their own vegetables. It teaches them to care and nurture, provides physical activity and a connection with nature. It makes them value how the vegetables they buy in the market have reached them. If they indulge in birdwatching and learn about migration of birds according to seasons, it again connects them to nature. They will learn about how birds know when seasons change and what route to fly and in which direction? If they dance to music, children will discover rhythm. They definitely need a connection to the real world; the digital world should not become their only reality.

DIGITAL DEMERITS

Staring at the computer screen for long hours can result in short sightedness. Students who watch TV most of the time get poor results academically.

Light and radiation from the TV can create an imbalance in hormone production, so one should never go off to sleep with the TV on. In 2005, hundreds of children in Japan were hurt by an unusually strong radiations from the TV while watching an animation programme, and required medical attention.

Increased television exposure can cause a change in DNA cells, resulting in cancer. It could result in sleep disorders and sleeplessness. As discussed earlier, obesity and poor social relationships are also a consequence. Neighbours and family members often quarrel if the TV is being watched at a loud volume.

It is, therefore, important to restrict time in front of the TV/computer screen, or else it can affect one's health and/or happiness.

HANDLING DIGITAL STRESS

When spending time in front of the TV/computer, children should do about fifteen minutes of exercises to avoid stiffness, to aid in digestion and to prevent depression. The areas where tension collects when working on the computer are the eyes, neck, shoulders, arms, back and legs.

When working on the computer a glare screen should be placed on the monitor and dusted daily. Anti-glare spectacles are also available, and can be worn when working on the computer. If you already wear spectacles, then you can get an anti-glare coating on them. Ideally, the monitor should be twenty degrees below eye level like a natural reading position, and at a distance of an arm's length from the child.

Both feet should be resting flat on the floor and the child should sit upright at a comfortable height. This prevents stress in the neck, shoulders and back. Neck and back pain can interfere with a child's sleep and performance at school. The discomfort can also make the child adopt a negative attitude.

Lighting should not be too bright, and there should be no glare or shadows on the screen. The curtains should be drawn to avoid glare. Lighting should be from the left side of the screen and not brighter than three times the light of the computer screen.

To protect the eyes from "locking" and to prevent the onset or progression of near-sightedness, every twenty minutes the child needs a visual break of twenty seconds. So every twenty minutes the child should look away from the computer screen for twenty seconds. He can look into the distance, rotate the eye-balls in a circle, clockwise and anti-clockwise five times, look up and down five times and side to side five times.

Motions from clicking the mouse or typing on the key board can cause carpal tunnel syndrome or pain in the wrists. To avoid this, the child should stand with arms stretched out in front of him and makes fists. The fists should then be rotated ten times clockwise and ten times anticlockwise. The fists should then be opened and both hands should be rotated from the wrists, clockwise and anticlockwise. After this, the fingers of both open palms should be spread as far apart as possible and held in this position for five counts. This may be repeated ten times. Now, as his arms remain outstretched, the child should clench both fists tightly, then release them, and repeat this ten times.

The child should then lift his shoulders up as close to his ears as possible then take them as far in front as possible, and the take them down as far as possible, and to the back as far as he can. This action should be done in one fluid motion, making circles with the shoulders. Repetitions should be five times in one direction and another five times in the opposite direction.

In today's digital age, parents face the challenge of helping their children strike the right balance between sitting in front of a TV/computer screen, or playing, exercising and social interaction, etc.

SEXUALITY AND CHILDREN

At a family wedding, there was much chatting, singing and dancing. There was an atmosphere of merriment and enjoyment. Children were running helter skelter, adolescents were huddled together in deep conversation, to be occasionally summoned to join in the singing and dancing to be performed on the day of the *'ladies sangeet'*. Suddenly, much to everyone's embarrassment, little Vivek and Rohan were on the floor. As Vivek lay down, Rohan sat astride him, and they mimicked what undoubtedly appeared to be motions of sexual intercourse!

Sometimes, children may innocently imitate sexual behaviour that they may have watched their parents may have to indulge in. With crowded living conditions, parents may have to indulge in sex when they presume the children are asleep. Unaware that they have been watched, they may be astounded when they see their child indulge in 'imitative' behaviour. Children have no idea that what they are doing is sexual behaviour.

SEX AS ENERGY

When it comes to our children, we should remember sexuality is perfectly normal. It is God's own gift to us, and we should be glad that our child's sexuality exists.

It is very difficult to take away sexuality from a human being. In Hinduism, it is the sexual energy which is symbolically referred to as energy (kundalini) that is made to rise from the base, or pelvic plexus (mooldhara) up through the centres of energy along the spine (the solar plexus, the heart plexus, etc.) to finally reach the divine energy centre located at the top of the head, or to the upper most region of the brain. All creativity and enjoyment are said to spring from this energy source.

Sigmund Freud believed that all activities of the world are based on sex, or libido. Likewise, in Hindu mythology, Lord Vishnu rests on the divine serpent; and Lord Shiva wears a snake around his neck, like an ornament. This cannotates that Lord Shiva and Lord Vishnu have not killed or suppressed sex, but befriended it and sublimated it, as a snake is supposed to represent sex.

SEX AND ADOLESCENTS

Parents should not immediately give in to every wish of their children. The habit of self-control in matters of sex spills over from other general habits of self-control. You can teach children self-control in other sensory matters like, satisfying the sense of taste, for instance, and this would help the child in exercising self-control in sexual matters.

When speaking with adolescents about sex, it should not be suggested minus love. Love makes sex meaningful, without love sex is only mechanical. A sublime attitude towards sex is the first step towards sex sublimation. Sex should not be recommended merely for sensual gratification, but as an extension of the expression of one's love for one's partner. Having intimate sexual contact should not be the basis of a relationship; it should instead be the culmination of a relationship when an appropriate partner has been found. A healthy attitude towards sex is very important for a person's sexual health.

One needs to educate adolescents about being responsible about sex. Since sex is a natural urge, children will definitely experiment with it at some stage in their lives. It is more likely to be sooner than later, due to a natural sense of curiosity or peer pressure. It would be appropriate to make children aware that casual sex, or promiscuity could land them in major trouble. They could contract sexually transmitted diseases, or HIV (human-immunodeficiency-virus), or land up with an unwanted pregnancy. The HIV infection, if acquired, leads to the breakdown of one's immune system, so one can catch any infection one is exposed to, be it TB, skin infections, etc. When that happens, HIV becomes AIDS (Acquired-Immuno-Deficiency-Syndrome). Sexually transmitted diseases can be treated with drugs, pregnancies can be terminated, but why put yourself through this, when the trauma can be avoided? All it requires to avoid all these unwanted complications is responsible sex.

An important part of responsible sex is educating adolescents about the correct use of the condom as a means of protection from unwanted pregnancies, HIV and other sexually transmitted diseases. Children should also be made aware that the friends who goad them towards free wheeling sex may not be there for them when they deal with their trauma! There is a sad case of a young adolescent boy who contracted HIV from a sex worker, when, on his friend's birthday, as a treat, he and some other boys treated themselves to a visit to the red-light area, and each of them had sex with a sex worker for as little as fifty rupees per head. The boy experienced immense trauma and was angry with his health professional parents for not warning him of such dangers.

SEX AND SOCIETY

Unfortunately, in today's world, where our basic instincts are often suppressed, and perverse sexual behaviour is often observed in movies, books, and there is uncontrolled access to pornography, it often warps and distorts attitudes towards sex and sexual behaviour. Increasingly one hears of sex crimes against women or children.

SEXUAL CHANGES IN TEENAGERS

It is our duty as parents to inculcate a healthy attitude towards sex in our children, and at the same time protect them from possible abuse. Children should be made aware that changes in their body are normal in teenage years and happen to every boy or girl. Some may experience the changes in their bodies a little early, and others, a little later.

While a girl's body becomes more rounded and curvaceous, she also starts mensurating. A boy's body starts producing sperm, erections start to happen, the penis enlarges, moustache and beard begin to develop and there is a change in the voice. Both develop thick pubic hair, and hair in the armpits. The changes in their bodies indicate that they are now able to reproduce and can have babies. With this knowledge, they will also need to understand that they now need to be fully responsible of their sexual behaviour/activities.

It is important that children are taught to accept these changes in their bodies as normal. They should be taught to respect these natural changes that occur in their bodies, and be happy that these changes will make them a man or woman, and usher their lives into adulthood.

It is important that they are allowed to freely mingle with the opposite sex, and treat both sexes in the same way.

SEX IN THE CHILD

Sexual behaviour starts rather early in life. Sometimes when little girls have just learnt to sit, they may be noticed rocking back and forth in a rhythmic manner. Such rocking stimulates the clitoris and gives a pleasurable feeling. Also, when children are exploring their bodies, in the course of the exploration they may chance upon their sex organ and discover that touching it results in a pleasurable sensation.

Then around the age of two years, children begin to wonder why male and female bodies are different, why their bodies are different from those of adults, why members of the different sexes wear different clothes and do different things. At this age children may check each other out by exploring each other. They may imitate sexual behaviour seen in movies. It is best to distract a child with some other activity when this happens; never scold or belittle a child. Do not label their behaviour as 'bad' or 'shameful'. Do not worry that your child is a pervert. If two children of the same sex are spotted doing this, it does not suggest a bent towards lesbianism or homosexuality. Most parents experience fear of perversion, shame, sadness and embarrassment.

Between the age of five and seven, children become very curious about sex. To camouflage their interest in a more socially acceptable way, they may make it into a game, like playing 'doctor-doctor'. Or else, they might actually check each other out by dropping their pants. It is best not to blame the child if this happens. The incident is not likely to be repeated if there is adult supervision at play. Downplay the incident if it happens. Do not blame a particular child. Casually ask your child about the game they played that day. Then phone the other child's parent about what happened. Mention it and decide on supervision in the future. If another parent calls you about your child, and blames your child, keep the conversation short. You could say, 'Listen, this is hard for both of us, I'll get back to you,' suggest supervised play.

MASTURBATION

Around two and a half years of age, a large percentage of children start masturbation. By handling and playing with their sex organs, children experience pleasure, and so They may indulge in casual fondling of the genitals or rhythmic self-stimulation. Children may masturbate because it feels good, because they may be bored, or because it relieves stress and comforts them.

Many parents are shocked when they notice such behaviour in children. However, it is important not to scold, threaten or frighten the child. Some parents may threaten the child that if he continues such behaviour his penis might fall off; it is best not to say this. Distract the child instead. Remember, as far as the child is concerned, he knows nothing about sex; s/he is only doing something that is pleasurable, like sucking the thumb, for instance.

Sometimes small children (age five to seven) may be noticed to masturbate too frequently. To cope with it, and to lessen the child's urge to masturbate, parents can indulge in comforting the child. For instance, at bedtime the child's forehead can be stroked or fingers run through the child's hair. Any activity that provides comfort will help. The child can also be made to lie on the stomach, and the neck, shoulders and his back massaged.

According to Dr Rodiger, excessive masturbation is often the symptom of another problem. 'If the child is compulsive, we have to look at psychological causes. It reflects anxiety on the child's part. This is their way of self-soothing, to feel safe.'

Dr. Johnson says that when children masturbate excessively, they often stop when parents initiate more physical contact by touching, holding or wrestling. He further says, 'Parents should also look at whether their child is getting enough exercise and stimulation. If a child continues to masturbate excessively and in public, it is important that parents seek professional help by consulting a psychotherapist.'

Some children embarrass parents by indulging in sexual self-stimulation in front of people. It is important not to look horrified and scold the child, to threaten him or spank him 'for this terrible behaviour' or call the child 'nasty'. Instead, just tell hlim it is not good manners to do it in public. Just like it is not good-manners to defecate or urinate in public. Do not suggest what the child is doing is evil. Just say that this is very private thing, and should not be done when there is company. At the moment that it happens, give a child a toy. Or put some toffees or something else like a new eraser or sharpener in the child's pocket. Or, suggest another activity like going out and playing or playing with blocks or some other favourite toy the child might have.

Remember, children are not 'lusting', as adults might interpret it. The child does not fantasise his actions along with masturbation as adults might. A child masturbates simply because it feels good and/or relieves tension. Do not make the child feel guilty. Feelings of guilt can carry over into adulthood and inhibit a person's sexuality or sexual enjoyment, making them inhibited, or restrictive.

PREVENTING SEXUAL ABUSE

In order to protect our children from being sexually abused, we have to make sure that they are not easily approachable. Abuse generally can happen when children, who are innocent and, therefore, vulnerable, can be accessed easily. We should instruct our children not to go out with or talk to strangers.

As the year 2006 drew to a close, Delhi was shocked by the killings and sexual assaults that happened in Delhi's satellite town, NOIDA, in a village called Nithari. When a little girl saw the pictures of the accused in the media, she spoke of a number of instances that the accused had approached her in the recent past. Her mother said she had not taken her daughter seriously. 'I thought she was making up stories.' At one time the little girl had been approached when she went to fill water at a nearby tank. The accused offered to help her and said he would drop her home. Just then, another woman stopped the two and threatened the accused after which he ran away. Another time, the accused went to her school and said he had been sent by her father. The child was stopped from going with him by the teacher. At yet another time she was accosted by a woman who was allegedly an accomplice of the accused. The woman volunteered to walk the little girl home. In the words of the little girl, 'I was walking with my brother and some children. Since I fought with my brother, I was some way behind the rest. Then this auntie stopped me and said she would take me home. However, she turned around and started walking towards Nithari instead.' This was when her brother turned around and took charge of the situation.

It is a good idea to tell a child that the area of the body that is covered by the vest and undergarments, is a private area, and adults should not be allowed to touch them there. Likewise, they should not touch any one in those areas, even if an adult tells them to. Of course, they should allow it when they are being bathed or when the doctor is examining them. If someone asks them to touch these areas or, touches them in an uncomfortable way in these areas, they should immediately say 'No' and run away, and tell someone. 'No', 'Run' 'Tell', should be the rule. To further protect children, little girls should be told to avoid being alone in a room even with known adults, especially of the opposite sex, with whom they feel uncomfortable.

They should also be told that if some one touches these private areas or kisses them in a strange, uncomfortable way, and tells them NEVER to tell any one, it is a bad secret to keep. The person touching them is wrong, because these parts are private.

If your child so much as hints or suggests that someone has been touching them in these areas, do not disbelieve your child. Take action immediately. If the offender realises he can get away with it, the abuse is likely continue. Besides the offender can go one step further and threaten the child physically or emotionally into compliance. Or, the offender can perpetuate abuse, which the child might start to enjoy. Sometimes the offender can 'bribe' the child with goodies like chocolates or special favours of some kind, like special outings, inorder to be able to continue such behaviour. Such children might get the idea that sexual favours can beget goodies. Or, guilt about the issue can set in and they can clamp up.

To avoid sexual abuse of your child, you should keep the following points in mind:

1. Supervision of children is important. If supervision is difficult you should put your child in playgroups where they are not alone.
2. Do not encourage children to kiss adults 'good night' or 'thank you.'
3. Discourage children hugging, kissing and sitting on laps of adults, unnecessarily.
4. Remember, opportunity plays a major role. If the offender stays in the same house as the child and has easy access to the child, it could result in abuse. So, be alert if your child ever mentions something suspicious.
5. The offender may load the child with gifts, outings or money. These should be grounds for suspicion, if, along with this, the adult and child spend a lot of unexplained time together.
6. You should teach children not to open the door to strangers, and to keep the door chain in place when accepting letters or parcels.

Another way that children can be protected is by not giving them too much too soon. Sometimes, when both parents work in order to earn a double income, they have tight schedules. They, therefore, do not mind giving in to the children's demands to compensate for too little time and attention they give them. Cash, mobile phones and cars are easily available to children today. When children have such facilities and are permitted to go where they like and do what they please, it is difficult for them not to stray, if values have not been instilled in them in their growing years. They live in homes equipped with internet connections, and there is no one to regulate what they watch on them.

Such children may quite easily start experimenting with sex, if they have not been educated earlier about the dangers of casual sex and the fact that sex should be accompanied with emotional attachment. Moreover, children have to be made to understand that some things are age specific. For example, it does not mean that if the parents are partying every day, the children can do the same.

SIGNS OF SEX ABUSE

Certain physical and behavioural changes that help ensure an early detection of abused children are:

1. The child displays a deep sense of loneliness and isolation.
2. The child exhibits depression, anxiety and withdrawal symptoms, adversely affecting normal childlike behaviour.
3. Bed-wetting, especially among little children, becomes more frequent.
4. The child tends to avoid a particular person/persons.
5. The child shows signs of difficulty in concentrating at school or in passing exams.

6. A sudden use of sexual vocabulary, which would be something alien to the child's social habitat.
7. Passing of blood when the child is passing stool.
8. Complaint of irritation in the throat, anal or genital areas by the child.
9. Recurrent bladder and throat infections could manifest in the child.
10. Symptoms of sexually transmitted diseases exhibited by the child.

HOW TO DEAL WITH SEXUAL ABUSE

Although the girl child is more susceptible to sex abuse, boys can also suffer sex abuse. Boys can be forced to indulge in anal or oral sex. In case your child has been subjected to sexual abuse, the first rule is to stay calm. Ask the child to explain what has happened, in his or her language. They may say, 'He played with my number one thing.' They may add 'It hurt', 'I didn't like it', 'He asked me to massage his body.'

When your child tells you about what you feel is sex abuse, never show shock. It could frighten your child into silence. Further, do not say what happened was good, bad, right or wrong. Do not blame or reject your child. For instance, if a young girl has been hugged or kissed by an uncle, do not insinuate that she in some way brought on, or encouraged that behaviour. Just ask the child to express in her own words what s/he feels. It is important that the child is able to sort out emotions and come out with what she feels, be it anger, hate, fear etc.

Hug and comfort the child—or show your affection in any other way, maybe by just holding her/his hand. Make it clear you love and support her/him in spite of what has happened.

After reassuring the child in this manner, make sure you completely block any communication or access of the abuser to the child. If the abuser is a friend or a relative, that person should be cut out of your life at once. Instruct your child never to open the door to that person. Further, confront that person with what he or she has done, no matter what the consequences. This way, you will prevent that person from unleashing such behaviour on other innocent children. At the same time, it will protect your child from further abuse.

An abused child may feel disgusted, shocked, humiliated, worried, confused, angry, fearful and/or guilty It is important to make the child feel loved and supported. It is very important for the parents to take a firm stand. That will considerably reduce long-term trauma to the child.

Do not be afraid to bring up the issue, since the offender can be anyone, even, embarrassingly, someone very close to you. Such offenders could be the father, brother, brother-in-law, cousins, neighbours, servants, teachers, coaches, friends, landlords, maids, etc., or anyone who the child knows well, apart from strangers.

TALKING TO CHILDREN ABOUT SEX

There is very little open talk of sex generally. A lot of what children pick up is from the attitude towards it, of the adults around them. We should sensitise our children to the loving and giving aspect of love that eventually goes with sex. Further, both parents should exude comfort and freedom with their bodies. There should be no feeling of disgust or embarrassment. When both parents are comfortable and at ease with their bodies, children sense their attitude and pick it up.

When discussing parts of the body, parents should use words like testicles, penis and vagina, not any slang associated with these. Slang makes children feel there is something about these parts to be ashamed of. The child should be told that this part of her/his body is called the vagina/penis, and that this is the part that makes her/him a girl/a boy.

When parents decide to talk of sex to their children, they often tend to take the help of a textbook on human reproduction. Instead, they should first explain to child that when two people like each other, they like to spend time together. When people who like being together are adults and of either sex, sometimes they get married. They then become very loving, gentle and nurturing towards each other. When they are together, they feel loved, wanted, cuddly and warm. At times, they get so close to each other that the penis is either very close to, or enters the vagina. From then on, the textbook can be used to explain that sperms escape from the penis to fertilise the ovum. The fertilization process can be explained further by saying that the ovum is like a seed in the female, the sperm is like water that helps the seed to release the plant, or, the baby, in this case.

You should talk of sex as an experience that stimulates the whole body. Sex should not be spoken of as just a baby-making process.

When you decide to talk about sex to your child, do so when you sense your child is ready to listen. If your child asks you a question about sex, you should only give information that the child is seeking at that moment.

Your child will only be able to ask questions on sex, and you will be able to answer such questions only if you have an open line of communication with your child. Comfortable communication is basic to good parenting. The best time for establishing open lines of communication with children is at bedtime. You should not attempt to communicate things when children are getting ready, eating a meal or doing homework. At bedtime, the atmosphere is relaxed. The parent is not distracted by other matters, and neither is the child. It is a good time for everyone to say their 'sorries' and 'thank yous' to each other. It is also a good time to share the joys and sorrows of the day. Only when you communicate about inane and mundane things, will talking about something as important as sex, be easy and natural.

PRECAUTIONS YOUNG GIRLS AND WOMEN NEED TO TAKE TO KEEP STALKERS AT BAY

Delhi police have prepared certain guidelines for girl and women to follow, so as to protect themselves:

- When coming home late at night, they should avoid short cuts that are not well-travelled or well-lit.
- They should know the proprietors of reputed neighbourhood stores which remain open late in the night and if they feel they are being followed, they should go there.
- When walking to the car or on the way home, they should keep their keys in their hand, till they are safely inside.
- If someone is droping them home, they should be asked to wait until the lady being droped is safely inside the house.
- While driving alone they should keep the windows rolled up and doors locked.
- If someone attempts to force them off the road, they should't panic, but blow the horn constantly to attract attention. If forced to stop, they should reverse the car and back away as soon as possible.
- If they are being followed, they should make a few random turns, if possible. If still being followed, they should head for the nearest police station, fire station or open store.

- They should park their cars in a well-lit area.
- Before getting into the car, it should be made sure that no one is hiding in it. The car should be always be securely locked when parked.
- If alone at home, they should have the key ready before they get to the front door of the house.
- If a stranger wants to use the phone for any kind of emergency, he should be kept out, and the call should be made by someone inside the house.
- If the main door is found open when one arrives home, under no circumstances should the house be entered. The police should be called immediately from the mobile phone, a pay phone or a neighbour's phone.

ENVIRONMENT

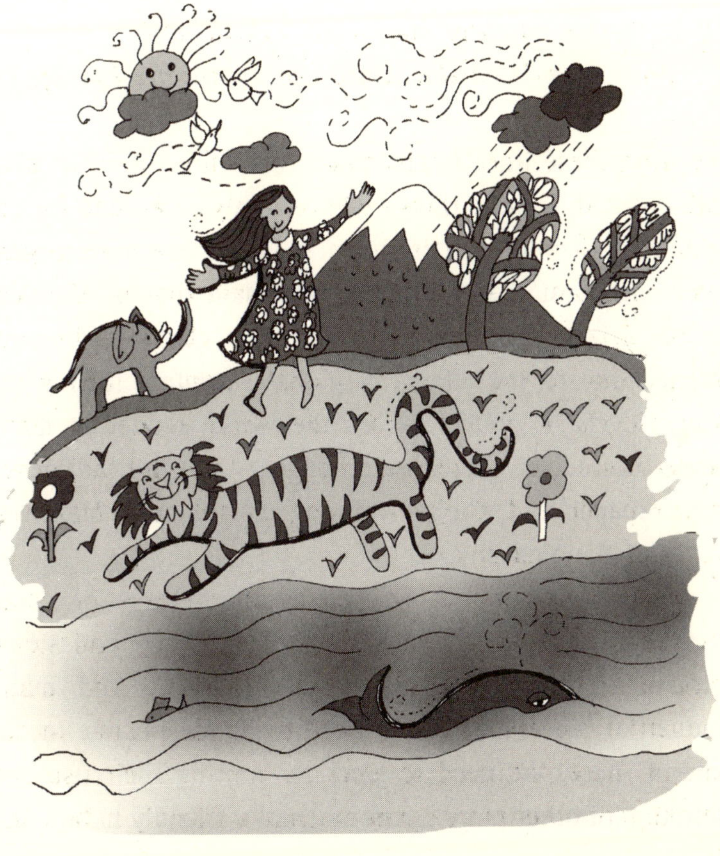

There is a very interesting quote by the French environmental photographer, Jacques-Yves Cousteau:

> *This is our hope:*
> *That the children born today,*
> *Still have twenty years hence,*
> *A bit of green grass under bare feet,*
> *A breath of clean air to breathe,*
> *A patch of blue water to sail upon,*
> *And a whale on the horizon to set them dreaming.*

Reading these lines might make you think that this is no tall order, that these things will certainly be around for our children. However, environmental issues are more urgent and important than we think. It is said that by the year 2050, a large number of icebergs and glaciers will have melted due to the effects of global warming, raising the water-levels of oceans across the world, rendering many areas around sea shores water-logged. A recent headlines in a newspaper read, 'Global warming can submerge Maldives, parts of Bangladesh.'

Global warming is caused by the release of gases into the atmosphere from aerosol cans, vehicle emissions, air-conditioning, styrofoam, power stations, and many industrial processes etc. We need to be responsible in our use of these. We need to work at limiting their use and thinking of other more environmentally friendly habits and technology. For instance, using public transport, walking or riding a bicycle, or, using solar energy, wind energy, etc. can go a long way in helping solve this problem. America, apparently, is the biggest environmental polluter in the world!

It is now officially recognised that it is human activities that are causing global warming, and not natural processes like volcanic eruptions or solar activity, etc. High up in the sky is a layer of oxygen called ozone, which forms a thick layer called the ozone layer. This protects us by shielding us from the harmful rays of the sun. It only allows the rays that are good for us to filter through and blocks out the rays that can harm us. Today, this ozone layer is being irreversibly damaged by man-made gases.

Plastic is another environmental hazard. It is non-biodegradable, and just continues to pile up in the environment, impervious to the effects of water and air. Plastic is being freely dumped into the environment, and it is said that this is one of the reasons that the reproductive health of polar bears has been drastically affected.

It is frightening to think that if you mix plastic with soil in a flower pot, nothing will grow in it! The plastic will prevent free passage of air and water to the roots, and worms that live in the soil and 'plough' the soil with their movement through it, aerating it, will die if they eat the plastic. There have been many instances of cows dying after eating plastic bags. Sometimes, they eat plastic while trying to get to the vegetable peals etc. packed in plastic bags and thrown either in the garbage or at roadsides.

It is important that we respect the environment, or else, as the philosopher Francis Bacon says:

'In nature things move violently to their place, and calmly in their place.'

The recent tsunamis that occurred in oceans worldwide, causing havoc and devastation are a case in point.

The cause of environmental protection needs to be taken up urgently by children. The reason being when their parents were children, there was no great concern about saving the environment. People were not aware that the environment was in trouble. They created a lot of garbage and environmental hazards unthinkingly. People waste energy (electricity/gas etc.), petrol and water without thinking twice, sometimes just for fun! These are treasures of the earth and must be used with discretion and care. Although adults know better today, they still have a lot of bad habits. That is because it is difficult to change habits once you are grown up.

The hope of saving the planet, therefore, rests to a very great extent on children.

Whether we are able to save the environment, or abuse it and further deteriorate it, will greatly affect our lives, the lives of our children and indeed, the lives of all future generations to come. So what strategies can parents and children adopt in order to save the planet?

WATER

Fresh, clean drinking water is getting increasingly scarce. It is the most precious resource that we need to preserve, without further delay. There is only about two to three percent drinking water left in the world. We must do whatever we can to stop depleting the remaining fresh water resources, by using it very carefully. One place where we can start saving a lot of water is our homes!

Believe it or not, the water that we flush down our toilets is fresh, clean, drinkable water! Old flush-tanks have a large capacity and use up a lot of water. There is a trick you can share with children that will help save water by reducing the amount of water your flush tank will use. Take a plastic water bottle of one litre capacity and fill it with water. Then screw on the cap tightly. Then lifting the lid of the flush tank, lower the bottle gently into it, avoiding to touch the mechanism that works the flush. Recover the tank, leaving the water filled bottle inside. The weight of the bottle will prevent the flush from filling to its full capacity, thus reducing the amount of water used each time the flush is used.

Apart from this the number of times the flush is used can be reduced by flushing the toilet after two or three times of passing urine. Children can use a bucket for bathing instead of a tub or a shower. Water should not be left running when brushing teeth or shaving. Hose pipes should not be used to wash cars. First, the car should be dusted with a dry cloth to get rid of most of the dust. Then use a bucket of water and a duster to wipe clean. Repair leaking taps, tanks or pipes immediately, and always look for leaks. Do not water the garden when the sun is high up in the sky, since you will lose water to evaporation. If you have a huge garden, invest in drip farming methods or water sprinklers in the garden to prevent wastage of water.

Rain water can be harvested and saved by transferring it to the water table. It can replenish the water table level, and be very useful in the dry months. Only thirteen percent of rain water in agricultural areas goes to the water table, the rest is either lost to evaporation or only wets the top layers of soil. In urban areas, even lesser water goes to the water table due to cementing.

If rain water harvested from the storm water drain of one house in the city is one to two lakh litres, water harvested from storm water drains of four to five houses will be thirty lakh litres!

So, community water harvesting is an important option. With coordinated community effort, we may well see dry bore-wells come alive and have the luxury of fresh clean water round the year!

LITTER

As mentioned earlier, animals can die if they eat plastic wrapping material along with food. Food thrown out of a running car can attract animals to it when they smell food, increasing their chances of being run over by on-coming traffic. Animals can cut their tongues from half-opened cans that have been thrown around.

Many animals get sick from eating cigarette butts, plastic reinforced disposable plates or styrofoam containers/plates/packing material.

Some years ago, the city of Mumbai experienced devastating floods. Investigations pointed to two major causes. One was that plastic had clogged drains and prevented water from being drained away! Second, was that buildings had been built right in the course of the Mithi river, so that during excessive rains, flood water inundated the city, instead of flowing out with the flow of the river.

Children and adults alike should realise that it is important to throw garbage in trash cans. When on a picnic, you should always carry empty bags for the trash you generate.

You and your child should talk about this to others to propogate a sense of cleanliness and environmental consciousness. Schools should be encouraged to organise awareness drives on this, too.

SHOPPING

World over, if everyone reused their plastic grocery shopping bags just once, it would half the demand for plastic bags! Remember, every little effort counts. You should never feel that your lone effort will not make any difference to the larger picture; it most certainly will. More importantly, you will also motivate and encourage others who want to do something, but hesitate to do so, because they are embarrassed to be different from the rest.

Bags are made from the earth's treasures. Paper bags are made from trees and plastic bags are made from oil derivatives. Manufacturing of both is pollution inducing. So, you and your child must say no to bags that you don't need. For instance, if you buy a packet of chips, you are given a bag which you promptly throw away! Later, you also throw away the bag from which you have eaten the chips. According to the 'Save a Tree' campaign, a fifteen-year-old tree would make about 700 paper bags. So, children should be tought to refuse a bag when they buy something small. They should carry their own bags when they go shopping. They could carry a backpack to put their shopping in, or a cloth or jute bag.

A child should also be taught not to buy things that originate from animal sources, for example, ivory, fur coats, corals, etc. Animals are often hunted and killed ruthlessly for these products, and this could lead to these animals becoming extinct! Extinction of certain species could create havoc with the delicate balance in the ecology in which we live.

PETS

As is commonly seen, people often keep dogs and cats as pets. A common problem with pets is that they could get ticks and fleas that live off them by biting them and sucking their blood. You can buy tick and flea collars to prevent these parasites from living on your pet. These collars mainly contain pesticides, or poisons. so they are as bad for pets and you, as they are for the ticks! Some of these chemicals are known to cause cancer. That is why most flea/tick collars carry warnings to caution you on how you should handle them and dispose them.

Besides, more fleas than the ones that are on your pet might actually live in your house! These may be living in rugs, electric sockets, cracks in the wall, floors or stairs. So when you try and get rid of the fleas and ticks from your dog, you should also try to get rid of them from your house.

Fleas drown in soap and water, so you should give your pet regular baths with soap and water.

A flea comb should be used on your dog. This is a comb that has teeth very close to each other, so that when you comb your dog's coat with it, the fleas get stuck in the teeth, and can be removed. Keeping a bowl of soapy water ready can be useful, so that you can dip the comb in it when you catch fleas. The fleas will drop in the water and die.

FUTURE OF GARBAGE

A hundred years from now, a piece of plastic buried in your garden can be discovered intact by your great-grandchild when shoveling in the garden. Imagine that!

As we pile the earth with more and more plastic (car-doors, buckets, bottles, CD and DVD covers, grills, disposable syringes, footwear, toys, television/refrigerator/bodies, etc., just to name a few) we will have so much plastic and hazardous chemicals in the earth (from household cleaners, antiseptic solutions, pesticides, lead from batteries, chemicals from industrial processes, oil from oil spills, etc.) that it might get difficult to grow food! We need to urgently address these issues and save the earth from an impending environmental disaster.

According to the book *Treasured Island* by Sunita Rao, here is a list of how long different kinds of garbage take to disintegrate:

Banana peel	–	3 to 4 weeks
Paper bag	–	1 month
Cotton rag	–	5 months
Woollen socks	–	1 year
Wood	–	10 to 15 years
Leather shoe	–	40 to 50 years
Tin can	–	50 to 100 years
Aluminium can	–	200 to 500 years
Plastic bag	–	1 million years
Styrofoam	–	An eternity!

One thing children can be taught to do is to reuse whatever is possible. A culture of reusing plastic bottles can be introduced in your community like the cosmetic brand Bodyshop has done, where people bring in their empty bottles to be refilled from a large dispenser. Children can favour buying cold drinks in glass bottles rather than plastic bottles, as glass bottles can be reused by cold drink manufacturers. Paper can be saved by using both sides of it, photocopying the exact number of sheets required, reusing sheets of paper, using cloth towels and dusters instead of paper for cleaning etc. Food can be carried in steel tiffin boxes rather than in plastic bags/aluminium foil/cling film.

BIBLIOGRAPHY

Canfield, Ken R.; *The 7 Secrets of Effective Fathers: Becoming the Father Your Child Needs*; Tyndale House Publishers, 1993.

Fromm, Eric; *The Anatomy of Human Destructiveness*; Henry Holt, 1992.

Hurlock, Elizabeth; *Child Growth and Development*; McGraw Hill, 2007.

Lewis, Paul; *The Five Key Habits of Smart Dads: A Powerful Strategy for Successful Fathering*; Grand Rapids, MI, Zondervan Publishing House, 1996.

Misra, Kamlakar; *Significance of Tantric Tradition*; Arddhanarisvara Publications, 1981.

Satter, Ellyn; *Secrets of Feeding a Healthy Family: How to Eat, How to Raise Good Eaters, How to Cook*; Kelcy Press, 2008.

Wurtman, Judith and Nina Marquis; *The Good Mood Diet*; Rodale Press; 2007.

REFERENCES

1. *Christian Parenting Today* magazine; March/April 1993.
2. *50 Simple Things Kids Can Do To Save The Earth*; The Earth Works Group.
3. *Readers Digest* (issues from the 1990s).
4. Osho Zen tarot cards.
5. New Our Bodies; The Boston Women's Health Book Collective.
6. *Treasured Islands*; Sunita Rao, Kalpavriksh & ANET
7. Writings by Daisaku Ikeda, president of Soka Gakkai International